Moon Signs

Picking the Right Time for Everything You Want to Do

by Sabine Heideweg

Sterling Publishing Co., Inc.
New York

Library of Congress Cataloging-in-Publication Data

Heideweg, Sabine.
[Immerwährende Kalender der Mondkraft. English]
Moon signs : picking the right time for everything you want to do / Sabine Heideweg.
p .cm.
Includes index.
ISBN 0-8069-1897-7
1. Astrology. 2. Moon—Miscellanea. I. Title.
BF1723.H4513 1999
133.5'32—DC21 99–20315
CIP

Translated by Hans-Jakob Wilhelm

10 9 8 7 6 5 4 3 2 1

Published by Sterling Publishing Company, Inc.
387 Park Avenue South, New York, N.Y. 10016
Originally published in Germany under the title
Der immerwährende Kalender der Mondkraft and

Distributed in Canada by Sterling Publishing
℅ Canadian Manda Group, One Atlantic Avenue, Suite 105
Toronto, Ontario, Canada M6K 3E7
Distributed in Great Britain and Europe by Cassell PLC
Wellington House, 125 Strand, London WC2R 0BB, England
Distributed in Australia by Capricorn Link (Australia) Pty Ltd.
P.O. Box 6651, Baulkham Hills, Business Centre, NSW 2153, Australia
Manufactured in the United States of America

Sterling ISBN 0-8069-1897-7

CONTENTS

PREFACE

The power of the moon works wonders. This is not a question of faith but of experience, and I can illustrate this with countless examples from my many years of practice as a psychological consultant. It is not only people with an especially romantic disposition who react to the moon. Its power affects everyone.

The moon travels into a different zodiac sign approximately every two and a half days. Finding the appropriate timing for many occasions big and small depends on how the power of the moon is influenced by the sign the moon is passing through at the time, as well as the phase of the moon and its position. In this book you will find everything you want to know on this subject. All you need to do is look up the thing you want to do—or heal—and you will find suggestions for the best time to go about it. If you want to plan a trip or a wedding, for example, to take place on a day when the moon will be working with you, you can start by looking up the dates when this will happen. Soon this perpetual calendar of lunar power will become one of your most valued resources.

Almanacs often list the phase of the moon in which to do certain kinds of gardening, but the effects of the moon are not limited to planting and harvesting. They apply to all important areas of life. It is up to us to understand the symbolism of the moon and to use its power effectively.

In the first part of this book you will learn how best to profit from the power of the moon in each of the important areas of life from A to Z. The second part deals with the significance of the individual lunar signs, so that you can determine for yourself how to use your energies most effectively. In the third part you will find lunar tables for the years 1920–1996, by means of which you can calculate the moon's position for past events. There as well you will find the lunar calendar for the years 1997–2020.

I especially want to thank Johannes Fiebig for his valuable tips regarding the use and interpretation of the power of the moon.

—Sabine Heideweg

INTRODUCTION

Phases of the Moon

■ THE FULL MOON

The full moon is the most exciting of the lunar phases. Many people have trouble sleeping when the moon is full. Sleepwalking is a common feature of this period. Some animals are restless; dogs bark through half the night. Herbs and roots harvested on this day will be especially effective. The number of victims of alcohol abuse also reaches its peak. More children are born during this than in any of the other lunar phases.

The main characteristics of the full moon are profound emotions and a noticeable restlessness. The moon and the sun are positioned directly across from each other in the sky and as far apart as they can get. Feelings of abandonment and other fears may present themselves, which do not necessarily originate in the present, but may resurface from previous times.

During the full moon, the earth's satellite reflects more of the sun's light to the earth than at any other time. Domains of darkness are suddenly illuminated. Repressed memories may appear, and ideas or desires that we have never had the courage to realize may make their presence felt.

While it is true that the period of the full moon is a phase of restlessness—and this might result in a delay in the processes of healing—how we evaluate this fact depends on our point of view. Of course, a sleepless night is not pleasant. But when forgotten wishes and fears reappear, or when new ideas and insights are born, it is often more important, healthier, and more worthwhile than undisturbed sleep.

The full moon, aside from all the agitation it creates, has from ancient times been thought the right time for an inner turnaround, for reconciliation and forgiveness, and for new friendships. It is also a time of solution and deliverance.

THE NEW MOON

The new moon makes itself felt less strongly, or at least less directly, than the full moon. It is excellent for new beginnings. Yet the darkness that accompanies the new moon awakens fears as well. You need the courage to step out into new spiritual territory in order to appreciate the new moon as a creative time. If you can muster this courage, the new moon will bless you with new powers. It will be as if your spiritual energies were being recharged and given another chance. If you want to rid yourself of problems, there is no better time than during the new moon. Whether you want to say goodbye to bad habits, to outgrown relationships, or to outdated beliefs, the new moon will support you in the best way. The new moon, of course, is also very appropriate for fasting and purification.

THE WANING MOON

When the moon is waning, its natural and spiritual powers are dwindling. Just as, when we're exerting ourselves physically, we need to exhale, so the waning moon supports us in deploying our energies. Among the wonderful secrets of lunar power is its ability to renew itself cyclically. That's why we do not have to fear a loss of energy when we exhaust ourselves in this phase. The moon is a mirror; it reflects the sunlight. And perhaps it is also a mirror in a figurative sense. It gives us back as much energy as we ourselves have invested.

The waning moon is a phase in which we can concentrate on life's essentials—what is useful and what is necessary.

THE WAXING MOON

New energies accumulate. Nature takes in, builds up, and strengthens itself. You may read that the waxing moon is above all a time for relaxation and recreation, but this is not necessarily the case. New natural and spiritual powers are maturing during the waxing moon. The soul opens further and further until the full moon is reached. You can now acquire insight into strangers, events in the distant past, or developments taking place beneath the surface of things. Nothing human is foreign to you when you take advantage of the opportunities offered by the waxing moon and the full moon. It is not always easy, but it is fulfilling and enriching when your soul grows wings.

The Position of the Moon

THE ASCENDING MOON

In the signs of Sagittarius, Capricorn, Aquarius, Pisces, Aries, and Taurus, the power of the moon is ascending. Ascending lunar power has a heightening effect. In human behavior it signifies growth and blossoming. In the house and garden, this is a phase of harvest and stockpiling.

THE DESCENDING MOON

In the signs of Gemini, Cancer, Leo, Virgo, Libra, and Scorpio, the power of the moon is descending. Descending lunar power has a deepened and deepening effect. In personal life it signifies maturity and harvest. In the house and garden it represents a phase of sowing and planting.

When the moon comes into Sagittarius, it is making a transition from descending to ascending power. Likewise, when it moves into Gemini, it is making a transition from ascending to descending power.

The lunar calendar gives no specific indication of whether you are dealing with the ascending or the descending moon, but you don't need that. Just check the lunar calendar to determine the position of the moon for each day, and then simply look up the sign, as spelled out above: for example, Pisces = ascending power; Virgo = descending power.

Moon Signs

As mentioned before, the moon remains in each sign of the zodiac for about two and a half days. When we say "the moon sign" we mean the sign of the zodiac through which the moon is passing at any given time. Using the tables on pages 127 to 155 you can easily calculate this sign for past and present events as well as future ones. It's fun to figure out the lunar signs of personal anniversaries, to see how they served—or didn't serve—you, and this can lead to rewarding insights. The sign of the zodiac in which the moon was located at the time of your birth is your personal lunar sign. The concepts "ascending" and "descending" have nothing to do with the waxing and the waning of the moon.

Over many centuries, key statements have been developed for the twelve signs of the zodiac. They are as follows:

Aries	I am
Taurus	I have
Gemini	I think
Cancer	I feel
Leo	I will
Virgo	I analyze
Libra	I balance
Scorpio	I desire
Sagittarius	I perceive
Capricorn	I use
Aquarius	I know
Pisces	I believe

The signs Aries, Leo, and Sagittarius belong to the element of fire; Taurus, Virgo, and Capricorn belong to the element of earth; Gemini, Libra, and Aquarius belong to the element of air; and Cancer, Scorpio, and Pisces belong to the element of water.

HOW TO PROFIT FROM THE POWER OF THE MOON
FROM A TO Z

HEALTH AND WELL-BEING

■ ACHILLES TENDON
The Achilles tendon is especially sensitive when the moon is waxing in Aquarius, but it can withstand more stress than usual when the moon is waning in Aquarius. This is true in the physical sense—while you're jogging or playing soccer, for example. But it is also true in the metaphorical sense, when dealing with a personal weak spot—your "Achilles' heel."

■ ACNE
Here we must pay attention to the moon in Aries. Treating acne is especially difficult when the moon is waxing, but very favorable when it is on the wane.

■ ALCOHOL
It has a stronger effect than usual when the moon is waxing. Be especially careful when the moon is waxing in Pisces!

■ ANKLE
The ankle is subject to the sign of Aquarius. *See* Achilles Tendon

ARMS

These are traditionally assigned to the sign of Gemini. During a waxing moon in this sign, strains and limitations are more pronounced than usual. Everything you can do to strengthen and care for your arms is most effective when the waning moon is in the sign of Gemini. The arms can reveal much about how relaxed or how tense you are. During the Gemini moon, be sure to pay attention to how you use your arms and how you relax them.

AROMA

When the moon is in the sign of Gemini, we are very receptive to fragrances and smells, and our power of discernment is especially pronounced. If you know your personal lunar sign, you can determine your personal aroma:

Moon in Aries	All spring flowers, rosemary, mint, carnations, cloves, lemongrass, vervain
Moon in Taurus	Lily of the valley, hawthorn, jasmine, lilac, cinnamon, apple, rose hip
Moon in Gemini	Vervain, iris, melissa, lemon mixtures
Moon in Cancer	Orchid, lilac, violet, water lily, strawberry, peach, tulip
Moon in Leo	Oleander, rose, hibiscus, pomegranate
Moon in Virgo	Sage, lavender, meadow flowers, pear, rue, hazelnuts
Moon in Libra	Apple, magnolia, avocado, carnation, cloves, plum, fennel
Moon in Scorpio	Anemone, thorn apple, cherry, sandalwood
Moon in Sagittarius	Marigold, herb mixtures, parsley, rosemary
Moon in Capricorn	Fennel, juniper, fir, dwarf pine, nuts
Moon in Aquarius	Narcissus, melissa, horsetail, snowdrop
Moon in Pisces	Fruit mixtures, herbs, amaryllis, crocus

■ BACK

This is regarded as the weak or blind spot of Leo!

■ BATHING

Bathing is especially relaxing during a waxing moon in the signs of water—Cancer, Scorpio, Pisces—and especially cleansing during a waning moon in these signs. Baths have a very calming effect during the days when the moon is in a water sign, and a stimulating effect when the moon is in an air sign—Gemini, Libra, or Aquarius. A bath taken while the moon is in a fire sign—Aries, Leo, or Sagittarius—will have the animating effect of an aphrodisiac, while it is always especially soothing and healing when the moon is in an earth sign—Taurus, Virgo, or Capricorn.

■ BEAUTY SLEEP

Beauty sleep is especially appropriate and beneficial during a waxing moon in the sign of Leo or Libra.

■ BELLY

Correlates with the sign of Cancer. The general rule is that when the moon is waxing you gain weight more readily than at other times. You gain less weight and are especially able to lose pounds, if you want, when the moon is waning. Both effects are greatly amplified when the moon is in the sign of Cancer.

Don't "wish away" your belly in accordance with the current ideal of beauty. Symbolically, the belly represents an important seam between upper and lower body, between head and feet, between body and soul. If there is a lot that you feel you have to keep together in your life, or as the person that you are, then this might also express itself in a large belly. As soon as you achieve this cohesion in some other way, your belly will become superfluous, and losing weight will not be a problem. So, by all means, care for your belly and pamper it.

■ BLADDER

Kidneys and bladder correlate to the zodiacal sign of Libra. If you have bladder problems, *see* Common Cold and Water.

■ BONES

The bones and the skeleton relate to the sign of Capricorn. Everything that benefits them is especially effective when the moon is waxing, but it is best to deal with the skeletal structure when the moon is on the wane in this sign.

■ BRONCHIAL TUBES

About half the experts hold that the bronchial tubes are related to the sign of Taurus, while the other half thinks that they resonate to Gemini. Until this dispute is settled, we must suppose that both signs are involved when someone suffers from bronchitis. Perhaps the bronchial tubes relate precisely to the passage between the signs of Taurus and Gemini, between throat and lungs, between head and body. And indeed, bronchitis is often the result of a contradiction between the head and the rest of the body, between theory and practice, or between will and necessity! Be especially careful with your bronchial tubes while the moon is in Taurus or in Gemini. If you want to strengthen your bronchial tubes to make them more resistant, this is best done during a waning moon in these two signs.

■ CHEST

Correlates with the sign of Cancer. It is interesting to note that in psychology the female chest is regarded less as a sex symbol than as a symbol of motherhood. Thus, the obsession with the naked chest that is cultivated by many magazines, psychologically speaking, reflects a kind of mother complex. The chest of females as well as of males, of adults as well as of children, is especially receptive to caresses during a waxing moon, and even more so when the moon is in the sign of Cancer or Capricorn. You can best alleviate illnesses or ailments of the chest during a waning moon in the sign of Cancer or Capricorn.

■ CIRCULATION

Circulation in general is influenced by the sign of Leo. When the moon is waning in Leo it is easier to forget circulatory problems; when it is waxing in Leo you have the opportunity to do something especially beneficial for your circulation. Blood circulation is related to Aquarius.

■ COMMON COLD

When you get a cold, first ask yourself what it means. This is more effective than fighting it blindly. In the case of a cold, the name already says a lot. Something has become "cold." Of course, you do not have to explain and interpret every little chill. But the more you are bothered, or even chronically haunted, by a cough, a runny nose, and so on, the more worthwhile it is to find out: What has become cold? Is there something—in your job or privately in your dealings with other people—that has lost its warmth and fire? It is useful to decide: What do you need to end, to say goodbye to, to let go of? And where do you need to kindle and feed a fire? The best time to find answers to these questions is during the moon's days in Gemini or Sagittarius, a time when the moon is changing from ascending to descending phases (see page 9).

Check the calendar to find out in what sign of the zodiac the moon was when your cold broke out. The sign will tell you the topic and the area of life in which you are able to bring cold and warmth, detachment and enthusiasm back into the right balance. Look for the cause.

■ CONSTIPATION

Usually this concerns less the bodily digestion than the readiness to let go of something. Constipation often points to pending changes in your life for which you are not yet prepared. Especially during a waxing moon, no matter which sign, work towards clearly expressing your rightful claims, while giving up futile attempts to hold on to the past.

■ COUGH

See Bronchial Tubes, Common Cold, Relaxation

■ DEPRESSION

Depression is especially heavy when the moon is in the sign of Cancer or of Scorpio. Wait two or three days until the sign changes, and the world will look different.

■ DETOXIFICATION, PURIFICATION

This is especially effective during a waning Virgo or Pisces moon, preferably just before the beginning of spring or before the end of summer.

DIARRHEA

The risk is especially high during a waning moon in the sign of Virgo. The waxing moon in Virgo, on the other hand, offers a good chance of alleviating or overcoming this ailment.

DIGESTION

Take special care of your digestion during the waxing moon in Virgo. During the waning moon in Virgo, however, the digestive system is rather robust and capable of processing even larger chunks. *See* Metabolism *and* Excretory Organs

DOCTORS' VISITS

There are no specific lunar rules governing doctors' visits, but the likelihood of being affected by particular illnesses or ailments is highest when the moon is in the sign that correlates with that particular region of the body. When the moon is in Taurus, for example, you may sense the state of your teeth or your throat especially clearly. In order to avoid additional stress, you might avoid treatments during these days.

But it is also true that when the moon is in the sign that correlates with the ailing part of the body, the helping and healing effects of the moon are especially noticeable. So, as long as no operation is performed or treatment carried out, a visit to the doctor can be beneficial on such a day.

You will find the information about which lunar signs correlate with particular parts or regions of the body in this chapter on page 30.

Choosing the right physician is often the best guarantee of successful treatment. Especially in larger cities, however, this can be quite difficult. When the moon is in the sign of Gemini, Virgo, or Aquarius, your chances of finding a suitable physician are particularly high.

DRINKING

At first glance, crying and drinking seem to have nothing in common. Yet both fulfill the same purpose: Things are flowing! It is better, however, to let tears flow than to reach for the bottle. And conversely, sometimes reaching for the bottle or glass can also be an attempt to comprehend your own feelings. The days of the waning moon in one of the three water signs—Cancer, Scorpio, and Pisces—are especially suited to changing and redefining your inner attitude. *See* Alcohol

■ EARS

Assigning the ears to a sign of the zodiac can be a complicated task. Often the ears are referred, along with the jaws, the mouth, and the throat, to the sign of Taurus. If we are talking about the power of listening—in the sense of empathy—then the signs of Cancer and Libra are involved as well. If we are talking about "listening to someone" in the sense of "obeying," this concerns Capricorn. And finally, the ear is also responsible for our sense of balance, which again involves Libra. Be sure to take all this into consideration when you have ear problems or problems of communication.

■ EDUCATION

As recent studies by French physicians have shown, the ability to fashion for yourself a picture of the world and to orient yourself in the world according to this picture is vital to spiritual and physical health. If you want to do something for your education, the best time to do it is while the moon is waxing in the sign of Sagittarius or Taurus.

■ EXCRETORY ORGANS

These fall under the sign of Scorpio. During a waxing Scorpio moon, they are especially sensitive. When the Scorpio moon is on the wane, they are most resistant.

■ EXERTION

An appropriate measure of work and exertion is necessary for health and personal well-being. Many counselors emphasize only tranquility and meditation, forgetting that human beings have a great need for meaningful activity and expending energy. Generally, you will be supported in this respect when the moon is in one of the fire signs—Aries, Leo, or Sagittarius. Miraculously, the energies of fire renew themselves by being spent. Especially during a waning moon in the three signs of fire, don't inhibit your drive towards activity.

■ EYES

The eyes have special significance for all three fire signs. The head and the face are ruled by Aries. Vision (the ability to perceive and identify something by means of the eyes) and facial care are Aries specialties. As the symbol of the sun and the heart, the eye belongs to Leo. The expression of the eyes, the visual power, and the direction of the gaze are related to the development of the "lion" in you. Sagittarius finally is characterized by intuition and strong personal beliefs, which in turn are related to ways and habits of seeing.

Measures taken for the purposes of eye care and the improvement of vision—or of the luminosity and radiation of the eyes—are especially effective when the moon is waxing in Aries, Leo, or Sagittarius. You might try an eye bath during this time.

When the moon is on the wane in Aries or in Leo, your eyes may need special care. A well-tried remedy that promises good results is parsley tea.

Rings under the eyes reveal, among other things, that the blood circulation in your face is partially blocked. The dark red congested blood shimmers through the delicate skin under your eyes. In order to stimulate the blood flow in your face, it is important that you look yourself and your current tasks straight in the eye. It is essential to remain in harmony with your own intentions. The power of the moon supports you in this on all the days when the moon is in a fire sign—Aries, Leo, Sagittarius—and of these, especially Sagittarius.

Bags under the eyes are either treated the same as rings, as signs of exhaustion, or as circulatory disturbances.

■ FACE

The face is interpreted as the mirror of your personality and, in particular, of your identity. Care is especially effective when the moon is in the sign of Aries or Libra. *See* Eyes

■ FASTING

The best time to fast is when the moon is on the wane and especially in the sign of Virgo. Sometimes the Scorpio moon is advantageous as well. Please try it for yourself. The days of a new moon are also particularly effective fasting days.

FAT

Fats like to gather especially when the moon is waxing in an air sign—Gemini, Libra, Aquarius. It is especially easy to get rid of fat when the moon is waning in an air sign.

FATIGUE

Especially during a waning moon in a fire sign—Aries, Leo, or Sagittarius—you could feel burnout. Every fire sign, however, is followed by an earth sign, which offers the best opportunity for personal regeneration.

FEET

The sign Pisces is responsible for the feet. The way you stand on your feet, how you run, and how you walk are, symbolically speaking, mirrors that reveal your attitudes. When the moon is waning, the feet are especially strong and trainable. All kinds of foot care work especially well when the moon is waxing in Pisces.

FINGERNAILS

Same as fingers, but in addition the moon in Libra or Capricorn has an effect that is especially helpful in the care of fingernails.

FINGERS

They are influenced most by the moon in Gemini. Care for them when the moon is waxing in this sign.

FRESH AIR

An essential factor in well-being, fresh air is especially needed and pleasant when the moon is in an air sign—Gemini, Libra, Aquarius. Be sure to take deep breaths and exhale thoroughly!

FRUITS

Unpicked, they grow best during the days when the moon is in the sign of Aries, Leo, or Sagittarius. The days it is in water—Cancer, Scorpio, Pisces—are best suited for eating the fruit. This can also be used as a metaphor for fruit of our labor or for personal fruitfulness. Clarity in our feelings and in our thoughts is only worthwhile if it can be realized in action. Achievements and activities can only bring happiness and satisfaction if they are fruitful in a personal sense—meaningful. In order to enjoy the fruits and make ongoing projects fruit-bearing, it is best to use water days.

■ GALLBLADDER

Gallbladder trouble could mean that you are too "venomous," or perhaps too aggressive. It could also be the case, however, that you need to defend yourself more effectively against aggression! For these purposes, the waning moon in Aries or Scorpio is especially useful.

■ GENITALIA

These are always assigned to Scorpio. You can rid yourself of genital problems especially easily when the moon is on the wane in Scorpio. Care, strengthening, and invigoration are most effective when the moon is waxing in Scorpio.

■ GLANDS

These correlate with the water signs—Cancer, Scorpio, and Pisces—not with air signs, as is sometimes claimed.

■ HAIR

The optimal days for cutting your hair are when the moon is in Leo or Virgo. If your hair is cut during a waning moon, it will grow back especially thickly. When grooming or cutting hair, it's better to avoid, if possible, days when the moon is in Cancer or Pisces. But don't let yourself become obsessed with these general guidelines. For many women, their personal cycle is what counts. Immediately after menstruation all forms of hair care, including coloring and styling, work better than at any other time.

■ HANDS

They need special care during a waning moon in the sign of Gemini; yet at that time they are also especially strong. Pay attention to the symbolic connections as well: To take something into your hands also means to grasp, touch, or comprehend something. The waxing moon in Gemini is the optimal time to take something "in hand" in this sense.

■ HEAD

Requires special attention during the days when the moon is in Aries!

■ HEARING

See Ears

■ HEART

All matters of the heart also affect your heart physically. This central organ is touched by all the issues that are really important to you—the issues that are "dear to your heart." The waning moon in Leo offers special opportunities to solve problems in this area. Steps to strengthen and revitalize the heart are especially effective when the moon is waxing in Leo. Express what is dear to your heart—get it off your chest!

■ HIKING

A life without movement is a life at a standstill, one that quickly diminishes in quality. Moving about in nature outside the city is especially recommended when the moon is in the sign of Aries, Taurus, Cancer, or Virgo.

■ HIPS

Some experts assign this area of the body to the sign of Libra; others assign it to Sagittarius. To be safe, pay attention to both signs if you should have problems in the hip or lumbar region. The waning moon is, as always, especially well suited for working out and settling problems, while the waxing moon is better suited for care and for taking steps to build up strength.

■ INTESTINES

Be especially careful during a waxing moon in Virgo.

■ JAWS

These are especially sensitive during a waxing moon in Taurus, and especially strong during a waning moon in this sign.

■ JOINTS

The joints are especially strong when the waning moon is in

Capricorn. They are especially sensitive when the moon is waxing in this sign.

KNEES

Symbolically, the knees represent steadfastness, self-assertion, flexibility, and humility. Special attention should be paid and treatment administered (bandages, knee-warmers, knee compresses), in the sign of Capricorn.

LEGS, LOWER

Positive as well as negative influences are especially noticeable when the moon is in Aquarius.

LIVER

Connected with the mythological character Prometheus, this organ is particularly influenced when the moon is in Sagittarius.

LOAFING

It comes especially easily and is especially agreeable when the waxing moon is in one of the three so-called summer signs—Cancer, Leo, or Virgo. Use these days to "hang loose."

LOSING WEIGHT

If you want to lose a few pounds, the best time to start is the first day after a full moon. For the following 12 days, the waning moon will support you in a pleasant and natural way. During this time, use every opportunity to contemplate the moon. It would be good if you could arrange it so that every evening you could at least glance at the sky. Even if you do this only for a few minutes at a time, you will sense how much the power of the moon supports you. On the basis of thousands of experiences we know that everything depends on your inner attitude and doing things at the appropriate time.

A special diet is not required, but it would help for you to eat soups, fruits, and especially vegetables. This will not hinder your purpose, and it will dispel the feeling of hunger. Only if you plan to reduce permanently will you be successful at losing weight.

In order to maintain your figure and continue to shape it while the moon is waxing, it is especially important to find a new orientation. In the days of the waxing moon you gather new ideas especially quickly. Begin to do this consciously one day after a new moon. If previously you had too much of something—namely pounds—then at the same time you had to be lacking something in a different area (tranquility, discipline, joy, or self-confidence, for example). To lose weight, you need to gain in those places where so far you have had a lack. No time is better suited for this purpose than the time of the waxing moon.

Be careful on days when the moon is in Cancer, Scorpio, or Pisces to watch your eating and snacking habits especially carefully. Pamper yourself on those days—but not with food!—and grant yourself a special wish. Days when the moon is in Gemini, Libra, or Aquarius are right for putting a little extra effort into losing weight.

■ LUMBAGO

This concerns the other side of the belly. Here we are also concerned with the question of your unity as a person, the connection between the upper and the lower body. Ruptures and contradictions between your wishes and reality are reflected in this area. You are especially affected by this when the moon is in the sign of Sagittarius. The waning moon in this sign provides good opportunities to rid yourself of specific problems, while the waxing moon is the right period to bring your wishes and reality into greater harmony.

■ LUNGS

The lungs are especially affected on days when the moon is in Gemini.

■ LYMPHATIC SYSTEM

The lymphatic system is especially affected and susceptible—in a positive as well as a negative sense—when the moon is in a water sign. The effect is especially long-lasting when the moon is in Pisces.

■ MASSAGE

Massage is effective in all the moon phases of Taurus, Virgo, Libra, and Capricorn. *See* Skin

MEDICATION

There is no global solution for the right use of medication. Much depends on your personal circumstances. *See* Doctors' Visits

MEDITATION

You can meditate not only when sitting still, but also during yoga or other exercises, and during any activity or business in your daily routine. Daydreams are an unconscious form of meditation. They can affect you when you are driving in your car, washing the dishes, doing office work, and so on. If you can handle this consciously, then you are in the enviable position of being able to use these daily activities for meditation purposes. *See* Relaxation

MENSTRUATION

In spite of sex education, menstruation is often a taboo subject in our society, one that is supposed to be hidden away. Amazingly, even some astrologers who celebrate the power of the moon and the resurrection of womanhood do not even mention a woman's menstrual cycle. Yet there is no clearer evidence of the power of the moon in daily life. This concerns not only the conscious female identity and the power of nature, but also the "voice of the blood," which ought to be listened to and understood. If you want to rid yourself of problems in connection with menstruation, or if you have special concerns, the days in which the moon is in Cancer and Libra are best for these purposes.

METABOLISM

The metabolic rate increases during the days of a full moon. Things proceed at a leisurely pace, on the other hand, during the days of a new moon, a time when it is better not to demand much of your body. Metabolism is an "alchemical" process in which solid substances are turned into energy and energies such as light and heat are built into solid substances. Especially effective in this respect are the days when the moon is in earth signs, which are also called the days of salt (*see* Nutrition). These days, however, do not just concern the metabolism of salt in the body, but rather the whole metabolism. During a waning moon in Taurus, Virgo, or Capricorn, you can purify your body especially well and energize your metabolism through nutrition and exercise. While the moon is waxing in this sign, all the vital substances and minerals that you introduce into your body have an especially lasting effect.

■ MOUTH

The lips, gums, teeth, and tongue relate to your sense of taste, your sensuality, and also your speech, your openness or withdrawal, and so on. They might reveal what you still have to chew on, what you still have to swallow, or what you might have to spit out. For better or worse, you can sense the effects of the moon especially vividly when the moon is in Taurus. And, by the way, it is no accident that the words "mouth" and "moon" have a similar spelling. Your personal obstinacy, feelings, and inner needs as symbolized by the moon also shape your mouth and your sense of taste.

■ NECK

Whether you are headstrong or stiff-necked, the neck plays a big role in your life and determines how you carry your head through life. Strengths and weaknesses in the neck area are especially noticeable when the moon is in Taurus.

■ NERVES

Days when the moon is in air signs—Gemini, Libra, Aquarius—count as typically nervous days. If you already have weak nerves, be especially careful during this period, especially if the moon is waxing as well. If your nerves are in good condition, however, and you need to master a difficult task where you need nerves of steel, days when the moon is on the wane in air signs will be most appropriate.

■ NOSE

Like the face, the nose is related to Aries. During a waning Aries moon, the nose is exposed to danger (*see* Common Cold). But you might also consider the old saying that you can judge the size of a man's penis by his nose. The face as a whole is often seen as a mirror of sex. The nose counts as a symbol of the male and the mouth as a symbol of the female. Considered in this way, a runny nose or other nasal problems do not necessarily point to Aries, fire signs, or the common cold. Sexuality—and therefore Scorpio—might be at play. When suffering from a chronic runny nose, protracted sinus problems, hay fever, and so on, ask whether sexual problems or sexual needs might be at the root of the problem. The days when the moon is in Scorpio are best for finding this out and for remedying the situation, if need be.

■ NUTRITION

Days when the moon is in a fire sign—Aries, Leo, Sagittarius—are called "protein days." Days when the moon is in a water sign—Cancer, Scorpio, Pisces—are "carbohydrate days." When the moon is in an air sign—Gemini, Libra, Aquarius—these are "fat days." When the moon travels through an earth sign—Capricorn, Taurus, Virgo—these are "salt days." Each of these nutrients has a particularly agreeable effect when the moon is waning. Negative influences and all nutritional "sins," however, can have an amplified effect when the waxing moon is in the corresponding sign.

■ OPERATIONS

If possible, it is important to carry out operations or surgical procedures during a waning moon. Furthermore, such procedures need to be avoided when the moon is in the sign that corresponds to the affected part of the body (see table on page 30). Emergency operations are of course exempt from this rule.

■ PAMPERING

When the moon is in Taurus, Libra, or Pisces, it is the right time for your personal pampering program. In a waning moon, you could be especially permissive in postponing certain unpleasant duties. In a waxing moon, it would be a shame if you didn't grant yourself one or another long-held wishes.

■ PARTYING

For many people, "making a night of it" is important to their well-being. Not only do we have a need for peace and tranquility but also for rapture and a break from the routine. For this purpose, the days of a waxing Aries moon or a waning Aquarius or Leo moon are especially suitable!

■ PERFUME

This is especially needed and effective whenever the moon is in the sign of Gemini. *See* Aroma

■ PIMPLE

See Skin *and especially* Acne

■ PREGNANCY

Personal fruitfulness is a basic issue for women and men in all walks of life. Pregnancy is in the end only one expression of this task and of the ability, shared by all of us, to make our own existence productive. Generally speaking, this involves, above all, the days in which the moon is in a water sign. With fertility, as with menstruation, general rules cannot take individual rhythms into account. There are many possible ways to make a life productive. Every working relationship requires a child, but this does not always have to be a physical child. Many projects lend themselves to a common goal. As Goethe says, "Only what is fertile is true." The question of fertility is one of personal truth and truthfulness. *See* Fruits

■ READING

If you take the time to read something, this does not only serve to inform and educate you. Reading also constitutes an act of intellectual concentration and at the same time of bodily relaxation. Your attention gathers to a focal point. This is why reading—as psychosomatic research has shown—is an important factor in personal stabilization. When the moon is in the sign of Gemini, Libra, or Aquarius, it is definitely a time to do some reading.

■ RELAXATION

There is a widespread belief that inactivity or laziness is the best way to relax. In fact, there are a great variety of factors that contribute to personal relaxation. When the moon is in a fire sign—Aries, Leo, Sagittarius—movement is especially conducive to relaxation. When the moon is in a water sign—Cancer, Scorpio, Pisces—you have the best chance of relaxing if you get your feelings in order and are able to flow in the desired way. When the moon is in an air sign—Gemini, Libra, Aquarius—relaxation is best promoted by developing new ideas and making decisions. In this case, personal clarity is the most important factor for achieving the appropriate degree of resilience, one which is neither tense nor slack. Finally, when the moon is in an earth sign—Taurus, Virgo, Capricorn—optimal relaxation is achieved by viewing the tangible results of your work.

■ REST

The optimal occasion for periods of rest are the days of new moon. *See* Relaxation

■ ROOM

Every person needs his/her own private living space where he or she can go to be alone and undisturbed by others. This is particularly noticeable during a new moon and in the signs of Cancer, Virgo, Capricorn, and Aquarius. On these days especially, you need a chance to withdraw.

■ SAUNA

Perhaps you will have noticed that a visit to a sauna can—at different times—have quite different effects on your body and your mood. The explanation for this is found in the different qualities of the days. A visit to the sauna will have a healing and strengthening effect on the days when the moon is in an earth sign—Taurus, Virgo, or Capricorn. A sauna will be stimulating and inspiring when the moon is in an air sign—Gemini, Libra, or Aquarius. A calming and cleansing effect is achieved during the days when the moon is in a water sign—Cancer, Scorpio, or Pisces. A sauna has the invigorating effect of an aphrodisiac—something that increases pleasure—when the moon is in a fire sign—Aries, Leo, or Sagittarius.

■ SHOULDERS

Sometimes it may seem as if you are carrying all the weight of the world on your shoulders (especially during a waxing moon in Gemini). Be sure to have a clear mind and clear thoughts so that when the moon is waning in Gemini you can make the necessary decisions and cast off the burden.

SKIN

The best days for skin care are the days of a waxing moon in Libra or in Capricorn. For facial skin, also look to Aries. In a larger sense, you might also use the days of Capricorn and Libra to consider what you need in order to feel comfortable in your skin now and in the future. All the earth signs—Taurus, Virgo, Capricorn—offer, especially during a waxing moon, ideal opportunities for needed bodily contact.

SLEEP

To get a full night's sleep now and again is very important for your health, and it's best not to limit this to the weekend. Even during the week you can arrange at least once to be undisturbed from the afternoon until the next morning. Days in which the moon is in Taurus, Cancer, or Pisces are best for this purpose. In this case, the waxing moon is just as favorable as the moon on the wane.

SMOKING

Some smokers are attached to their habit because of a sucking reflex. This involves the mouth and the sign of Taurus. Smokers have a special craving for a cigarette during a waxing moon, and a good opportunity to kick the habit during the days of the waning moon. For other smokers, intellectual work and nervousness are among the primary motives. This involves air signs—Gemini, Libra, Aquarius. These signs let smokers feel their addiction to nicotine more strongly while the moon is waxing, and can open up the possibility of breaking the habit while the moon is waning.

STOMACH

The waxing Cancer moon strengthens the stomach, while the waning moon relieves it. Drink chamomile tea and find out what is troubling you. Make sure that it is not things you "can't stomach"—and angry feelings that are giving you a stomachache. You are especially sensitive, but also very resourceful, during a Cancer moon.

STRESS

There is a healthy kind of stress that is necessary for life, and an unhealthy kind of stress that can be very harmful. Days when the moon is in a fire sign—Aries, Leo, or Sagittarius—are best suited for separating these two kinds of stress, especially when the moon is waning in Aries or in Leo. *See* Exertion *and* Relaxation

SUN

One of the basic needs of human beings is for light and sun. Many people seek the sun in exotic vacation spots and in tanning salons. Yet we already carry quite large supplies of energy within us. A shortage of energy does not necessarily indicate a lack of power. A lack of goals or of worthwhile tasks can be involved as well. When the moon is in the sign of Leo, it is the best time to find your way to the sun within you, to your center, and to your heart. When the sun is in Sagittarius, it is the optimal time to find new goals and worthwhile tasks in life.

SWEETS

A symbol for the sweetness of life, which has to do with the right connection between body and soul. Days when the moon is in a water or earth sign are especially effective in this connection. Taurus is said to have a sweet tooth, and a special preference for nibbling. When the moon is on the wane in Taurus, ask yourself whether you might have a pent-up demand for sweet things in your life; and especially when the moon is waxing in Taurus, be on guard against uncontrolled nibbling.

TEARS

Tears are as healthy and beneficial as laughter. And they are recommended for men as well as women, especially during a waxing moon in Cancer or Pisces, and during a full moon.

TEETH

These fall under the sign of Taurus (with influences from Aries and Capricorn). Whatever benefits or hurts your teeth has a stronger effect on the days when the moon is in Taurus. If you are already uneasy about a visit to the dentist, then, of course, do not choose a Taurus day for such a visit. If, however, in your case, the objectives of pain relief and healing are more important, then even a Taurus day may be favorable.

■ THIGHS

These are affected and make themselves felt especially in the sign of Sagittarius.

■ THROAT

Especially affected in the sign of Taurus.

■ THYROID GLAND

While most authors correlate the thyroid gland with the sign of Gemini, a few of them think it belongs to Taurus. When the moon is in the sign of Gemini, you will be most successful in affecting your thyroid gland. Go easy on it during a waxing moon, and be especially watchful during the days of a full moon.

■ TOES

The feet as a whole are especially in need of care and treatment when the moon is in Pisces. The best time to take care of your toenails is when the moon is in Pisces or Capricorn. Especially suitable for clipping your toenails: the waning moon in Capricorn.

■ UTERUS

The uterus is connected with some aspects of sexuality, femininity, and motherhood, which correlate to the sign of Cancer. Care and healing during a Cancer moon are especially strong when the moon is on the wane.

■ VEGETABLES

These are especially needed and especially delicious when the moon is waxing in the water signs—Cancer, Scorpio, and Pisces.

■ VEINS

Influences of any kind are more noticeable when the moon is in Aquarius.

■ WATER

Many people now are making it a habit to drink a glass of water about every hour throughout the day. You will promote your well-being, your vigor, and your general productivity by stirring up the liquids in your body. Especially on days when the moon is in a water sign—Cancer, Scorpio, Pisces—and then particularly during a waning moon—keep a large jug of water next to you. An occasional visit to a lake or to the sea will also serve your well-being. Ideal for this purpose are, of course, days when the moon is in a water sign, and also the days of a full moon.

WEIGHT GAIN

Although diets for the purpose of losing weight generally arouse the most interest, there are actually quite a few people who want to gain weight. The waxing moon offers the best opportunity. If you begin one day after a new moon, you will have almost 14 days ahead of you during which the waxing moon will support you substantially. Be sure to maintain your weight in the subsequent phase of the waning moon so that, if need be, you can gain more in the phase after that.

WEIGHT LOSS

See Losing Weight

Signs Ruling Individual Parts of the Body

Aries	head, brain, face, nose, forehead
Taurus	throat, neck, mouth, vocal chords, teeth, jaws, tonsils, ears, larynx
Gemini	shoulders, arms, hands, lungs, bronchial tubes, breath
Cancer	chest, stomach, belly
Leo	heart, blood circulation, eyes, back
Virgo	intestine, digestive organs, spleen, pancreas
Libra	kidneys, bladder, ovaries, uterus
Scorpio	genitalia, excretory organs
Sagittarius	thighs, legs, hips
Capricorn	knees, bones, joints, skin, pelvis, coccyx
Aquarius	lower legs, veins, autonomic nervous system
Pisces	feet, toes, heels

GARDEN AND NATURE

APPLES

Apple trees, like all fruit, do well when planted and cared for during a waxing moon. The right signs for this purpose are Aries, Leo, and Sagittarius. When the moon is waning in these signs, it is also a good time to prune the fruit trees and shrubs.

BALCONY PLANTS

Balcony plants that are not watered by rain should preferably be watered on "leaf days"—when the moon is in Cancer, Scorpio, or Pisces.

BEANS

Beans belong to the category of fruit plants. They grow best when cared for and cultivated on "fruit days"—when the moon is in Aries, Leo, or Sagittarius. It is best to eat beans when the moon is in an earth sign—Taurus, Virgo, or Capricorn—when they are especially easy to digest.

BERRIES

Planting, sowing, and cultivating are best done during a waxing (or during a descending) moon on a "fruit day"—when the moon is in a fire sign—Aries, Leo, Sagittarius. Eating the fruit is most appropriate on fruit days, when you are particularly receptive to fertility and the fruits of life, as well as the days when the moon is in a water sign—Cancer, Scorpio, Pisces.

BIRDS

Days in which the moon is in the sign of Virgo, Libra, or Aquarius are especially suited for dealing with these beautiful, indispensable feathered friends.

CABBAGE

Cabbage is counted among the flower plants and develops best when planted and cultivated on a "flower day," when the moon is in an air sign—Gemini, Libra, or Aquarius. As always, the ascending moon (Sagittarius, Capricorn, Aquarius, Pisces, Aries, or Taurus) is best suited for harvesting.

■ CARROTS

Like all root vegetables, carrots appreciate being cultivated on a "root day," when the moon is in Taurus, Virgo, or Capricorn.

■ CATS

The cat is our friend and a bit of "animal nature" in our house. You will get along best with your four-legged friend when the moon is in the sign of Aries, Libra, or Aquarius.

■ CAULIFLOWER

Interestingly enough, cauliflower belongs to the flowering plants, that is, to the plants whose "fruits" develop like flowers. Here the rule is that the most favorable time for care and cultivation is a "flower day," when the moon is in one of the air signs—Gemini, Libra, or Aquarius.

■ CELERY

Celery grows best if planted and cultivated on a "root day"—when the moon is in Taurus, Virgo, or Capricorn.

■ CHERRIES

Cherries grow especially well when they are cared for and cultivated on "fruit days"—Aries, Leo, and Sagittarius. They have a particularly sensual quality when eaten during a waxing moon.

■ COMBINATION PLANTING

Try the following: planting carrots with onions, tomatoes with onions, tomatoes alongside parsley, lettuce alongside radishes, peas with celery, potatoes alongside cabbage. When you do this, please observe the following basic rules: All plants that grow above the ground should be planted, sowed, and cultivated during a waxing (or descending) moon. Plants that grow underground flourish best when you sow or plant them during a waning moon. If necessary, you can also sow and plant during a descending moon.

■ COMPOST

It is ideal to set up your compost heap when the moon is on the wane. Further filling and compacting can then be done during a waxing moon. As an alternative time for setting up a compost pile, consider the descending moon. Try it. If you stick to these time periods, you will have good compost at your disposal much earlier. Add biological composting catalysts on days when the moon is in an earth sign—especially Virgo, but also Taurus and Capricorn. As with all applications of fertilizer, compost should be spread during a full moon or a waning moon.

■ CUCUMBERS

Cucumbers belong to the fruit plants and grow best if they are cultivated on "fruit days"—Aries, Leo, and Sagittarius. It's best to eat them during days when the moon is in a water sign—Cancer, Scorpio, or Pisces—when they are especially easy to digest.

■ CUTTINGS

The time of a waxing and descending moon, and especially when the moon is in Virgo, are excellent for getting and working with cuttings.

■ DOGS

The dog is important as a friend, as well as a domestic animal. On the days when the moon is in Taurus, a dog is especially ready for training and for unusual activities.

■ DOMESTIC ANIMALS

It is not only the garden that brings a part of nature into your life, but also domestic animals. This is especially noticeable when the moon is in the sign of Taurus, Cancer, or Capricorn.

■ FAT

The best time to take in fat, when the human organism needs it most and when it is easiest to digest, is when the moon is in an air sign—Gemini, Libra, or Aquarius.

■ FERTILIZER

First, determine whether fertilizer is really necessary, and if so, how much fertilizer is best for your plants. Break with the habit of applying excessive amounts, and take the time to figure out the right measure across several periods of growth. The right amount of fertilizer is one issue; the right time to apply it is another. If at all possible, fertilize during a full moon or a waning moon. Flowers should be fertilized (and watered) on "leaf days"—when the moon is in Cancer, Scorpio, or Pisces.

In the case of flowers with weak roots, you can choose "root days"—Taurus, Virgo, and Capricorn—in between the "flower days," which can help them along a little. The best time to fertilize grain, vegetables, and fruits is on "fruit days"—Aries, Leo, and Sagittarius—during the waning moon or the full moon. On days when the moon is in Leo, be particularly careful, since there is the danger that the soil and the plants will dry up. With the moon in the sign of Leo, artificial fertilizer could easily burn the soil and the seeds!

■ FLIES

Flies cannot be avoided in the garden. In the house, curtains and fly nets are best installed on a day when the moon is in an air sign—Gemini, Libra, or Aquarius.

■ FLOWER DAYS

These are days when the moon is in an air sign—Gemini, Libra, or Aquarius.

■ FLOWERS

Assuming that you are primarily interested in beautiful flowers and not so much in the roots and leaves, then "flower days"—when the moon is in Gemini, Libra, or Aquarius—are best for all activities of care and cultivation. Here again the general rule proves valuable: All plants that grow above the ground should be planted, seeded, and cultivated during a waxing (or during a descending) moon.

■ FRUIT DAYS

These are days when the moon is in a fire sign—Aries, Leo, or Sagittarius.

■ GARDEN DESIGN

Besides the regular garden chores, once a year it is wise to set aside some time for planning your garden. The days of the waxing moon in Aquarius are especially appropriate for this purpose. It will remind you that the garden is an important symbol. The way you shape it, and the way you wish and imagine it to be landscaped, are reflections of your personality. The garden as a whole falls under the sign of Virgo.

■ GOALS

See Sky Watching

■ GRAFTING

The optimal time is the waxing moon, especially close to the full moon and on a "fruit day"—Aries, Leo, or Sagittarius.

■ GRAIN

Grain is a fruit plant and is especially grateful for the care you give it on "fruit days"—Aries, Leo, and Sagittarius. Apply fertilizer only during a waning moon.

■ HARVESTING

The most favorable time for the harvesting and preservation of fruits and vegetables is the time of the ascending moon, that is, when the moon is in the sign of Sagittarius, Capricorn, Aquarius, Pisces, Aries, or Taurus. Don't forget to leave a bit of produce in the garden or on the field as a gift of thanks.

■ HEDGES

The optimal time for clipping hedges is the waning moon. It would be good if it were also a "leaf day," but generally every sign during a waning moon is suitable. If you cannot find time during a waning moon or if the weather does not cooperate, you can choose a sign of the descending moon (Gemini, Cancer, Leo, Virgo, Libra, Scorpio) to help you carry out the clipping as easily and effectively as possible.

■ HERBS

The ideal time for the planting and cultivating of herbs is on a "flower day"—Gemini, Libra, or Aquarius. The right time for the harvest is the time of the ascending moon: Sagittarius, Capricorn, Aquarius, Pisces, Aries, or Taurus.

Another rule, even though it is one that partly deviates from the principle just mentioned: An herb heals and helps especially well if it is harvested in the moon sign that corresponds to the body part upon which the herb is supposed to act. On page 30 you will find a table that tells you which parts of the body belong to each moon sign.

■ HOUSEPLANTS

Basically, they are treated according to kind and variety in the same way as outdoor plants. It is important that they are not watered or fertilized too much. Here too the day that the moon is in Virgo is ideal. *See* Watering *and* Fertilizer

These grow best when they are sown and cared for on a "root day," when the moon is in an earth sign—Taurus, Virgo, or Capricorn.

■ INSECTS

Insects are beneficial in the control of lice and other pests, as well as indispensable for the pollination of plants. If you are dealing with insects, days when the moon is in the sign of Gemini or Capricorn are most suitable.

■ LEAF DAYS

Leafy plants that are not watered by rain should be watered on these days—when the moon is in the sign of Cancer, Scorpio, or Pisces.

■ LEEKS

Leeks grow best if you care for them during "leaf days"—when the moon is in Cancer, Scorpio, or Pisces.

■ LETTUCE

"Leaf days"—when the moon is in Cancer, Scorpio, or Pisces—are the right time for planting and cultivating lettuce. Note that lettuce is an exception to the rule that plants growing above the ground should be planted and sown during the waxing moon.

MEDICINAL HERBS

The same rules apply for most medicinal herbs as for flowers: They grow best if cared for and cultivated on "flower days." Those are the days when the moon is in the sign of Gemini, Libra, or Aquarius. For gathering medicinal herbs, *see* Herbs.

NATURE AS SYMBOL

Many experiences in or with nature have a symbolic significance. External nature is a mirror image of inner nature, and the garden is an ancient symbol for a world that can become a paradise for human beings. In order to allow your own nature to develop fully, it is helpful to ask yourself what your personal goals are—or what your personal "paradise" might look like. Go into a garden, or at least out into the open, when the moon is in the sign of Libra, Sagittarius, or Pisces. This will be an excellent time for gaining clarity about your goals and the next steps to take towards attaining them.

PARSLEY

Especially rewarding and digestible is parsley, if cared for during "leaf days," when the moon is in Cancer, Scorpio, or Pisces.

PEARS

Pears are especially tasty when the moon is in Cancer or Virgo. *See* Apples

PEAS

They belong to the fruit plants. Care and cultivation benefit them most on "fruit days"—Aries, Leo, and Sagittarius.

PESTS

You will often see houseplants infested with aphids as a result of excessive watering. If possible, do not water plants except on "leaf days"—when the moon is in Cancer, Scorpio, or Pisces. At least on "flower days"—when the moon is in Gemini, Libra, or Aquarius—refrain from any watering at all.

Pests, and especially aphids, often infest plants that have been watered on "flower days." Suddenly exposing houseplants to rain can have just as negative an effect. The leaves are not used to direct contact with water and can become diseased or attract pests. Outdoors, help is provided against these unwanted visitors by ladybugs and other insects.

The waning moon is suited for all applications of pest control. The optimal time to eliminate pests that live in the soil is during a "root day"—Taurus, Virgo, Capricorn. For the control of pests living above the ground, the signs of Cancer, Gemini, and Sagittarius are especially suited.

PLANTING

The ideal time for planting is when the moon is in the sign of the descending moon: Gemini, Cancer, Leo, Virgo, Libra, or Scorpio. Note that all plants growing above the ground (except lettuce) are to be planted during a waxing moon, while all plants growing underground are to be planted during a waning moon.

PLANTS GROWING ABOVE THE GROUND

These should be planted or sowed during a waxing moon or during a descending moon. The one exception is lettuce. The best time for the harvest is during the ascending moon (in Sagittarius, Capricorn, Aquarius, Pisces, Aries, or Taurus).

PLUMS

For the purposes of cultivation, be sure to observe the "fruit days"—when the moon is in Aries, Leo, and Sagittarius.

POLLEN

The fact that more and more people are suffering from "hay fever" and reacting allergically to drifting pollen may be seen as a sign of our alienation from nature. In the short term, you can protect yourself effectively if you are especially careful during "flower days" (when the moon is in Gemini, Libra, or Aquarius). The best long-term protection, however, is not to spend less but more time out in nature, until you have so accustomed yourself to it that the allergy begins to recede. Here, take note of the fact that external nature is a metaphor for the nature within. An allergic reaction against external nature also signifies a lack of harmony in your own inner nature. Perhaps you have major desires that are insufficiently recognized or disturbing problems that are provoking your allergic reactions. The ideal time for finding answers to these questions is the waning moon in an air sign—Gemini, Libra, or Aquarius—as well as during the new moon generally.

■ POTATOES

As with all plants that grow underground, here too the waning moon is the right time for planting. You should make sure, however, that planting does not occur too close to the new moon. The seedlings develop much better just after the full moon. Try planting potatoes when the moon is in Pisces!

■ PRESERVATION

When the moon passes through an ascending sign—Sagittarius, Capricorn, Aquarius, Pisces, Aries, or Taurus—it is appropriate to preserve the yields of the harvest.

■ PROTEIN

We require and digest the greatest amount of protein when the moon is in a fire sign—Aries, Leo, or Sagittarius. The waxing moon is especially suited for building up muscle mass and physical strength. The waning moon in a fire sign pays the highest rewards for the use of physical strength. At these times it pays to exert yourself a little.

■ PRUNING

Plants should be pruned during a waning moon. If for some reason this is not possible, a descending moon (when the moon is in Gemini, Cancer, Leo, Virgo, Libra, or Scorpio) is also an appropriate time.

■ RADISHES

Like all root vegetables, radishes are grateful for treatment on "root days"—when the moon is in Taurus, Virgo, or Capricorn.

■ RAIN

Like the sun and the moon, like wind and weather, it is wise to become acquainted with and befriend the rain. This is important so that you do not feel like a stranger when you are outdoors, but are just as much at home as inside. Days when the moon is in a water sign—Cancer, Scorpio, or Pisces—are especially suited for this purpose.

■ ROOT DAYS

Here we are dealing with days when the moon is in one of the earth signs—Taurus, Virgo, or Capricorn.

■ SEEDLINGS

These grow optimally if they are set into the ground when the moon is in Virgo. If that is not possible, make sure to do it during a waxing moon, or at least during a descending moon—Gemini, Cancer, Leo, Virgo, Libra, or Scorpio.

■ SKY WATCHING

As you examine your plants attentively and follow their development and growth, you might also get in the habit of observing the sky with devotion and patience. The point of this, of course, is not only to inform yourself about the development of the weather in the next hours or days. Rather, it is that by observing the sky regularly you will gain a new familiarity with nature and the environment. The continuous observation of the heavens will give you the sense of being at home even out there. Especially right for this purpose are the days when the moon is in an air sign—Gemini, Libra, or Aquarius.

■ SLUGS

There are various methods and recipes for controlling slugs. Whatever path you choose to keep these unwanted visitors away from the garden, the right time for controlling them is the waxing moon in Scorpio.

■ SPINACH

As with any leafy vegetable, the "leaf days," when the moon is in a water sign—Cancer, Scorpio, or Pisces—will be most helpful for planting and care.

■ STORAGE

The time of the ascending moon—Sagittarius, Capricorn, Aquarius,

Pisces, Aries, or Taurus—is the ideal time for putting things in storage, as it is for harvesting and preservation.

SUBTERRANEAN PLANTS

Plants growing underground develop best if they are sown or planted during a waning moon. If for some reason this should not be possible, you can also choose a day with a descending moon—Gemini, Cancer, Leo, Virgo, Libra, or Scorpio.

TRANSPLANTING

The best time is the waxing moon, regardless of the sign it happens to be in. If this is not possible, choose the descending moon—Gemini, Cancer, Leo, Virgo, Libra, or Scorpio.

TREES

All plants that grow above the ground should be planted or sowed during a waxing moon, or at least during a descending moon. Plant care should also occur during a waxing moon. The annual cutting of plants should take place during a waning moon or, alternatively, during a descending moon—Gemini to Sagittarius. If you want to graft a fruit tree, do it during a waxing moon that is, preferably, close to a full moon, and on a "fruit day"—when the moon is in Aries, Leo, or Sagittarius. If the growth of a tree leaves something to be desired, cut the tips during a new moon just above a side branch.

TURNING THE SOIL

Repeatedly turning the soil is certainly desirable, especially with new patches, but often it is not feasible. If you are only able to turn over the soil in your garden once, do it during a waning moon in Capricorn. If you are in the fortunate position of being able to work on a patch several times, first turn the soil during the waxing moon in Leo, then during a waning moon in Capricorn, and finally for a third time again in Capricorn or, if that is not possible, in another sign during a waning moon.

VERMIN

For all methods of vermin control, the waning moon is the most suitable time. Vermin living underground should be treated on a "root day" (when the moon is in Taurus, Virgo, or Capricorn). If you want to combat pests living above the ground, you will be most successful when the moon is in Cancer, in Gemini, or in Sagittarius.

WATER

A garden without a body of water is like a meal without a drink. Whether it is a small pond or an elaborate water garden, you will derive much pleasure from it. The days when the moon is in a water sign—Cancer, Scorpio, or Pisces—during a waxing moon are especially well suited for creating and maintaining a water garden.

WATERING

All plants in enclosed spaces need to be watered in moderation. As with the use of fertilizer, people have a tendency to water too much. The slogan should be "Less is more." When watering your houseplants, limit yourself as far as possible to the "leaf days"—when the moon is in Cancer, Scorpio, or Pisces.

WEATHER

See Sky Watching *and* Rain

WIND

See Rain

YEARLY CYCLE

The rhythm of the moon is part of the larger cosmic course of events that is reflected in, among other things, the earth's yearly cycle. The major points of the year are the beginning of spring (the spring equinox), the beginning of autumn (autumnal equinox), the summer solstice, and the winter solstice. An important date in the cycle for yearly planning is February 2 (Candlemas or Groundhog Day).

CAREER AND FINANCES

■ ADVERTISING

The moon in Pisces or Aquarius is optimal.

■ BALANCE SHEET

The best time to prepare your balance sheet is when the moon is in Capricorn. The full moon in Capricorn is ideal, even if it occurs in the middle of a period, rather than at the beginning when the calendar changes as well. The moon in Libra is, of course, favorable for all issues of balances. Under the influence of the Scorpio moon you have the best chance of tracking hidden problems in the area of finance. The moon in Aquarius is most likely to reveal new possibilities to you.

■ BANKING

We are more critical and skeptical in our financial affairs during a new moon than during a full moon. For making investments, choose the waxing moon in Cancer. For taking out a loan, choose, if possible, the waning moon in Cancer.

■ BANKRUPTCY

A conscientious audit of your own business and of your business partners offers you the best protection. For this purpose, the right time is the waxing moon in Virgo, the waning moon in Pisces, or the waning moon in Scorpio.

■ BEGINNING WORK

The ideal time is the waxing moon in Aries and also every new moon, especially in its transition to a waxing moon.

■ BRAINWORK

By brainwork we mean theoretical, intellectual, mental, as well as volitional work, contrasted with manual labor. The moon is favorable for this purpose when in Aries or in one of the three air signs—Gemini, Libra, or Aquarius. During a full moon in Aries, however, be extra careful.

BUDGET

If you plan your budget when the moon is in the sign of Taurus or Virgo, you will be able to manage well with it.

BUSINESS TRIPS

If the moon is in the sign of Gemini, Leo, or Aquarius, it is an appropriate time for your business trip. The waning moon is especially suitable for clearing up open questions and settling old problems. The waxing moon, on the other hand, will support you when you take up new projects and develop innovative ideas.

BUYING

Shares, takeovers, and other business purchases are best dealt with when the moon is in the sign of Taurus. It would be ideal if you could do this during a full moon in Taurus!

CAREER

You have the best chances when the moon is in the sign of Capricorn. You are best able to spend your energies and complete ongoing projects successfully when the waning moon is in Capricorn. And you may confidently strive for new heights when the waxing moon is in Capricorn. Consider as well that there are many different kinds of careers.

CLAIMS

Many observations support the idea that during a full moon we are more liberal and reckless in dealing with money. During the time of the new moon, on the other hand, we are rather careful and skeptical. If you have claims to make or to defend, Aries, Taurus, and Scorpio will certainly help you in every lunar phase, but especially when the moon is waxing.

COMPLAINTS

Every complaint submitted to you is an offer to cooperate. When the moon is passing through Leo, Libra, or Sagittarius, you are not only able to handle complaints diplomatically, but you can even turn them into new and profitable business deals. If you yourself have the need or desire to complain, the right time is when the moon is in Virgo.

COMPLETION OF WORK

The waning moon in Virgo is the ideal time to finish up a work project. The new moon is also good, regardless of the sign it's in. From a religious or spiritual point of view, the waning moon in Pisces lends itself well to the completion of a larger work project. The full moon in transition to a waning moon is also suitable.

CONFERENCES

The optimal time is always when the moon is in an air sign, preferably in Gemini or Libra.

CONTACTS, NEW

It is of course possible to make new contacts at any time and on any day, but the waxing moon in Aquarius is especially helpful.

CONTRACTS

For this purpose, the moon in Libra, Capricorn, or Aquarius is the absolute best.

CONTROLLING

The best time for this purpose is when the moon is in Capricorn or Aquarius. All days when the moon is in Virgo are favorable as well.

DEBTS

If these are incurred as a result of sensible investment decisions, and are thus an expression of entrepreneurial spirit, the right choice is a time when the moon is in Aries or Leo. On the other hand, if the debts date back to inherited liabilities and are associated with feelings of guilt, you are most likely to find help with the waxing moon in Capricorn or a waning moon in Pisces.

GOALS

Suitable goals and real tasks are not only an important component of a high quality of life, but they also represent considerable personal capital, since they can bundle various energies and interests. You will make the greatest progress in this area if you use the power of the moon in Sagittarius, especially where Sagittarius changes over into Capricorn.

IDEAS

If you need a pioneering spirit, go for the moon in Aries.

If you are looking for the most productive use of existing resources and experiences, you will be best served by the moon in Taurus.

If the problem so far has mainly been a lack of creative ideas, you will most likely find help with the moon in Gemini.

If what has been lacking is individuality and taste, you are most likely to find your ideas in the sign of Cancer.

If you have been lacking in courage, on the other hand, you will make the greatest progress when the moon is in Leo.

If your analyses so far have been too imprecise, the moon in Virgo will be the right time for the innovations you are looking for.

If the old solutions just do not seem good enough anymore, it is the moon in the sign of Libra that will help you find better and more refined solutions.

If you want to rid yourself of superficialities and instead increase the effective depth or intensity of your actions, the appropriate time is when the moon is in Scorpio.

If your solutions and assessments are not far-reaching enough, the moon in Sagittarius is certain to bring you the best ideas.

If you are very ambitious and you want to bring your dormant talents up to speed, your optimal choice is the moon in Capricorn.

If you are looking for unconventional methods and truly astounding novelties, stick with the moon in Aquarius.

If you are looking for answers to very far-reaching questions concerning your global goals and other profound matters, you will be at the cutting edge in the sign of Pisces.

IDENTITY

Your identity is at the core of every success in your life. Here you are able to show outwardly what moves you inwardly, and what happens outside finds an echo inside you. This capacity for a productive resonance between the inside and the outside world—between yourself and other people—can be developed and experienced most clearly when the moon is in the sign of Cancer or Sagittarius.

INHERITANCE

The chances of an inheritance and the charges bound up with it can be recognized most clearly when the moon is in the sign of Capricorn or Libra. You can use this power in one of two ways: when you are about to inherit something, and when you are thinking about setting up your own will.

INTERVIEWS

The moon in Aries (waning) or in Libra (waxing) presents the best conditions. *See* Self-Portrayal, Presentations, and Self-Worth

INVESTING

The optimal times are the waxing moon in Virgo and the waning moon in Aquarius.

INVESTMENTS

With the moon in Taurus, and perhaps also with the moon in Aries or Aquarius, you will achieve the best results. If it is a matter of concluding old business deals, then pay attention to the waning moon in Taurus. If you are planning investments for the future, count yourself lucky if you can execute your plans during a waxing moon in Taurus.

LIQUIDITY

Just as money has more than one meaning, the question of liquidity too has different dimensions. The right time for securing or improving liquidity, if it concerns your economic mobility, is the waxing moon in Virgo. If it concerns prestige and influence, it is the waxing moon in Gemini; if it's the flow of energy and the power for continued movement that is needed, it's the waxing moon in Sagittarius; if it concerns personal security and satisfaction, it's the waning moon in Pisces.

MANUAL LABOR

As contrasted with brainwork. The days of the waning moon are ideal for all types of work that demand a lot of physical strength and energy.

■ MANUFACTURING

If you have something to produce or manufacture, choose the moon in Taurus to do it. If it is a matter of tackling new dimensions and bringing them into concrete form, then select Capricorn when it is activated by the moon.

Sources of error are most easily eliminated when the moon is in the sign of Virgo. You will find opportunities for improvement without much effort when the moon is in Libra. You will achieve the most elegant results when the moon is in the sign of Scorpio.

■ MONEY

The three earth signs—Taurus, Virgo, and Capricorn—are best for all types of monetary transactions. Yet money has a variety of meanings. If, for example, you are concerned with personal prestige, which you want to express through money or which you want to achieve through money, then days when the moon is in an air sign (Gemini, Libra, Aquarius) will have special significance for you. Quite a few people, on the other hand, regard money as a form of energy—they have certain goals and they use money in order to move something. If this applies to you, you will achieve the most when the moon is in a fire sign (Aries, Leo, Sagittarius). If money is supposed to offer you peace and security, however, you will fare best if you make your plans and your decisions when the moon is in a water sign (Cancer, Scorpio, Pisces).

■ NEGOTIATION

The optimal time is the moon in Libra.

■ PRESENTATIONS

Your demonstrations and presentations are unrivaled when the moon is in Taurus, Libra, or Sagittarius. Give it a try.

■ REAL ESTATE

Sell during a full moon; buy during a new moon. Or sell during a waning moon and buy during a waxing moon. Taurus, Virgo, Aquarius, and perhaps also Leo will offer you the best opportunities.

RESEARCH

Scorpio is especially thorough (particularly during a waning moon). Taurus is exceptionally persistent (especially during a waxing moon).

SALES

The greatest success can be achieved during a waning moon in Taurus.

SAVING

For this purpose, the moon in Capricorn is ideal. Yet the power of the moon in the sign of Taurus or Virgo is favorable as well.

SELF-PORTRAYAL

Smugness is a trap. But portraying yourself with clear expressions of your motivations and goals is an art form that you will find easier to master when the moon is in the sign of Taurus or Cancer.

SELF-WORTH

Having a clear sense of your own value, and of the value of things as well as ideals that are close to your heart, is indispensable for mobilizing great amounts of energy for long-term goals and tasks. Without such a sense, you will lack a sense of conviction at the moment when you need it, and degenerate into a working robot. Of course, it takes time—often a long time—to work out the values that have personal significance for you. Capricorn is ideal for these purposes, both in a waxing and a waning moon. The moon in Libra, Scorpio, or Sagittarius is also a very favorable time.

SHOPPING

Shopping is best when the moon is waxing in the sign of Taurus. You will be pleased with the great buys you can make.

TAX CONSULTANTS

With respect to the balance sheet, the moon in Aquarius is suitable for right relations with tax consultants. As far as accounting is concerned, the moon in Virgo is the best choice.

TAXES

Avoid the days of Cancer and Sagittarius when you are dealing with tax authorities. Days when the moon is in Taurus or Leo are more suitable and promise more success.

YEARLY PLAN

The optimal time for an annual plan is the time before and after New Year's Eve until February 2, and also the time just before the spring equinox (about March 20). The moon will support you especially when in the sign of Libra, if it is waxing, and in the sign of Pisces, if it is waning.

FAMILY AND CHILDREN

ADVENTURE

There are people who seldom stay at home. Especially during a full moon and when the moon is in a fire sign, they are overcome by a great restlessness. Actually, fire signifies movement, and when the moon is in Aries, Leo, or Sagittarius, these individuals must move, must move others, must be moved, must join movements, and so on. When the moon is in one of these signs, you need to open yourself to the flow of things. On the other hand, it's not true to say that adventures are only to be found far from home, or that fire and adventure do not go with rest and family life. Use the days of a new moon especially to resolve inner tensions and find more adequate solutions. If you're a person who never feels the need to break out, you might use the days of the full moon and the waxing moon of the fire signs in order to risk more adventure in your life.

ANCESTORS

Our ancestors influence our ideas. As far as these inherited, sometimes unconscious beliefs and expectations are concerned, you will do well to examine them when the moon is in the sign of Scorpio. But if the question in your mind concerns the value and the actual estate of an ancestor, the moon in Capricorn will help you to deal with the inheritance.

AUNTS

See Uncles and Aunts

BAPTISM

Every child who is born should be personally welcomed and celebrated. For this purpose, you do not necessarily have to go to church and organize a baptism. You can have various private ways of celebrating the birth. The right time for this is when the moon is in Aries.

BIRTHDAYS

If, on your birthday in the current year, the moon is in Aries, there's a good chance that you'll enter new spiritual territory.

If your birthday coincides with a moon in Taurus, the new year of your life will be particularly productive.

If your birthday coincides with a moon in Gemini, new things will be discovered and explored in your immediate vicinity.

If the moon is passing through the sign of Cancer on your current birthday, you will have a very good chance of finding peace with yourself in the new year.

If the moon is in the sign of Leo, the new year will bring crucial tests and greater willpower.

If the moon on your birthday is in the sign of Virgo, the new year promises to be a good one, if you bring order into your life.

If the moon on your birthday is in Libra, you will be more sensitized to vague feelings and novel ideas.

The moon in Scorpio emphasizes that what counts, especially in the coming year, is what you really desire—what you desire with the goal of eventually being happy without desire.

With the moon in the sign of Sagittarius on your birthday, you will tackle or achieve important goals and great tasks in the new year.

In the sign of Capricorn, on the other hand, the moon indicates that in the new year you need to return to your roots, because there you will discover new values and new talents.

The birthday moon in the sign of Aquarius means that in the new year you will live your life very conscientiously and be able to realize and achieve various interests.

In the sign of Pisces, the moon on your birthday indicates profound and rich feelings in the coming year.

BROTHER

The best time for dealing with your brother is when the moon is in the sign of Gemini. In the sign of Aries you are most likely to emphasize your autonomy with respect to him. And in the sign of Sagittarius, it is easiest for you to pursue your own plans and goals. In psychology and in the interpretation of dreams, a brother or sister is also a symbol for the alter ego, the other or second self.

CARING FOR THE SICK

Every position and every sign of the moon is suitable, because care must, of course, be given when it is needed. But it is important to have a practical empathy, the "right touch" in dealing with the sick. Especially when the moon is in the sign of Virgo, you will have good ideas about healing the sick, ideas that you can put into practice. You will always have exceptional empathy, and also the necessary distance with respect to the patient, when the moon is traveling through the sign of Pisces.

CELEBRATIONS

Of course, there are established holidays, but besides these, there should also be spontaneous celebrations. Good news, beautiful weather, special achievements by family members—there are many good reasons and beautiful occasions for celebration, and you'll be most likely to find them when the moon is in the sign of Gemini, Leo, or Libra.

CHRISTMAS

In our cultural sphere, Christmas is one of the most important family celebrations. At this time, the sun is in the sign of Capricorn. Your Christmas preparations and your Christmas experiences will turn out especially well if, at this time, the moon is also in Capricorn. The sign of Capricorn has to do with the "art of inheriting." Try to remind yourself of this art of inheriting as you look at the lights of the Christmas tree, and especially at its sparkling top.

CONFIRMATION/FIRST COMMUNION

Today, the religious significance of this event is often secondary. It doesn't signify an initiation into adulthood, either. Rather, what we celebrate is the independence of the offspring who have now ceased to be children and moved into adolescence. The moon in Gemini is favorable for difficult as well as for positive life experiences. *See* Puberty

As far as your own consternation is concerned, it is clearly the moon in Scorpio within us that is not only able to deal with this issue, but returns to it again and again.

DESIRE TO HAVE CHILDREN

Here too, Leo rules.

FAMILY GOALS

More and more people are making a conscious decision in favor of having a family, and against continuing their lives as single people. A study by a well-known research institute established that less than half of the couples interviewed claimed that tradition and convention played a role in their decision to form a family. For the others, there existed definite family goals. These research results would seem to make a lot of sense. There are many motives for forming a family. The moon in Aries, for example, can strengthen the pioneering spirit that searches for and realizes new ways of family life.

With the moon in Taurus, on the other hand, you can appreciate the value of family life: The powers of a person living alone add up. The powers of a person who lives with others multiply!

"If you value tradition and history, a sense of family and customs, it is as if you are creating your home on a mountain: You stand on the shoulders of your ancestors and find yourself united with many people besides yourself. The person who disregards tradition and convention emphasizes his own light, his own personal value, and his uniqueness. But as long as he or she stands alone, the light will remain low, no matter how brightly it might burn. The happy combination consists in a combination of both components, of tradition and individuality. When you carry your light onto the mountain of what already exists, then your light will shine in a wide circle. You will have a great aura and a superb outlook."

—Johannes Fiebig and Evelin Bürger

Family may also be important just to be able to find yourself; if so, the moon in the sign of Gemini can help, for without dialogue (the strength of Gemini), without "Ping-Pong energies" between partners, relatives, and neighbors, your own activity may become dormant.

When the moon is in the sign of Cancer, its proximity to the "inner child" reveals that your self-realization and continued development as an adult are not curtailed when you share your life with children, but are in fact enriched.

When the moon is in the sign of Leo, the play instinct is emphasized, an important adjunct to family life.

An essential family goal is the attempt to do things better, trying to correct the mistakes and faults of the past. This is best done when the moon is in the sign of Virgo.

The moon in the sign of Libra is good for dealing with life in communities. At the same time, it assists in the awareness of a personal completeness that is part of the goal of the family: Man becomes himself only through others.

With the moon in Scorpio, you may find it easier to access a deep connection with the secrets of life, and understand that all life revolves in a cycle of birth, death, and rebirth, which determines the basis and goal of family life.

The moon in Sagittarius emphasizes the thrill of adventure and also the learning experience that is a primary family goal. Here, just as in the sign of Taurus, parents can learn with their children, including new things when the children bring knowledge home from school.

With the moon in the sign of Capricorn, you can deal with the "art of inheritance." We all stand on the shoulders of our ancestors. And Capricorns are often deeply impressed by the truth that they have inherited the earth from their parents, but only borrow it from their children.

With moon in the sign of Aquarius, you will be receptive to everything that is new and recognize the truth of the saying "Only the person who believes in the future believes in the present!"

"Man only plays where he is man in the full sense of the word, and he is fully man only where he plays."

—Friedrich Schiller

The moon in Pisces, finally, is excellent for the great spiritual connection that provides the impetus as well as the goal of family life.

FAMILY LIFE

The twelve qualities represented by the signs of the zodiac are of course also reflected in family life. All desires as well as all fears in connection with the family can probably be attributed to the fact that so many issues of life come together here. Family life can suffocate in a routine. A loved and desired family life, on the other hand, is an expression of a high quality of life. It is easiest to shape it when the moon is in the sign of Leo or Pisces.

FAMILY REUNION

The waxing moon in Gemini and the waning moon in Pisces are ideal times for a family reunion.

FAMILY SECRETS

There are two kinds of family secrets. One type is known to all the members of the family, who make sure that the secrets don't escape to the outside world. These secrets have a negative character; they concern abuses and a disturbing state of affairs in the family circle. It is critical to remove the basis of such secrets, and perhaps reveal them to the outside world. The most important thing is to escape the spell of these family events. This will work best if you trust your own strength, which will be supported especially by the moon in the sign of Aries, Taurus, or Leo. Even more important is the ability to detach yourself spiritually and strengthen your personal immunity and independence. It is never too late for that, and it is always the right time. The lunar power gives you additional support when the moon is in the sign of Cancer or Aquarius.

The second type of family secret concerns qualities within a family that individual family members are not aware of and which thus remain "secret." Think of qualities such as affection, empathy, care, mutual responsibility, respect for the individual, curiosity regarding the development and growth of not only the children, but also the adults. These are values that are not guided by outward achievements or possessions. Here it is important to break out of the spell of the family secret by becoming more aware of your own values.

This is not an easy task, but one that is necessary and wonderful. For these purposes, the lunar powers work most favorably in the signs of Libra and Scorpio, as well as during a full moon.

FATHER

Every experience and confusion regarding your own father, the role of the father, and generally the image of fatherliness is felt most strongly and can also be dealt with most easily, when the moon is in the sign of Aries.

FATHER-IN-LAW

He represents an "other" or "second" father and may become a symbol of all that is negative or missing in the experience with your own father. You will be able to arrange all relevant issues optimally when the moon is in the sign of Aries or Capricorn.

FIRSTBORN

From the point of view of the parents, the birth of the first child represents the most significant break in the normal rhythm of life. A child enters what was until now a partnership between adults, and with this a family is born. The dynamics and profound repercussions of this event are perhaps paralleled only much later when the last child moves out of the parental home.

With the birth of the first child you enter unknown territory. You may have entertained many thoughts about it, but had no truly adequate picture. In the phase of life initiated by the birth of the first child, you will acquire additional personal powers when the waxing moon is in Aries.

FIRST DAY OF SCHOOL

The beginning of elementary school constitutes for children one of the most important first steps in their appropriation of the world and in their efforts to establish their own lives. For the parents it is often the first major act of letting go, but also a liberation from a permanent routine of care and entertainment. The beginning of school does not just concern a particular day, but should be experienced as an important new stage of life. The moon in Taurus will give you excellent support in this regard.

■ FRIENDS

The moon acts upon all the beautiful experiences with friends as well as the necessary confrontations. As always, the waning moon supports spending energy on the resolution of problems or muddles. The waxing moon supports the gathering of energy to put to use in a growing understanding of your own needs and those of your friends.

■ GAMES

As family psychologists have discovered, games are at the heart of family life. Neither the daily routine nor mutual care provide a durable and satisfying foundation of family life. Games create the essential bond between the members of the family, and this goes for sociable games as much as jokes, word games, and all expressions of the imagination and of joy. In this respect, the moon has the strongest effect in the sign of Leo. *See* Family Goals

■ GRADUATION

The best time for parties and celebrations in honor of this event is during a waning moon in Gemini.

■ INFANTS

Baby care and affection for children are one thing. It is quite another to be able to truly empathize with a young person, especially when it is not your own child. This capacity for empathy is important and necessary for appropriate relations with our youngsters. But it is just as important to understand and care for our "inner child," and the childhood memories and persistent needs we all carry within us. The moon in the sign of Capricorn or Cancer is especially well suited for this purpose.

■ MEALS

This is where family life takes place. Make sure that this meeting of the family is kept free of organizational and other tasks as much as possible. For such purposes, it's better to have a small discussion before or afterwards, so that the meal itself as well as the fellowship during the meal can be truly appreciated. Sharing a meal has an important and beautiful meaning. The best time to experience this is when the moon is in Pisces.

■ MOTHER

The best times for all beautiful experiences—as well as all necessary confrontations—with your mother, with your own role as a mother, and with the role that others play as mothers—are when the moon moves through Taurus, Libra, or Pisces. Grappling with many of these questions throughout your life, it is essential to continue to develop and redefine your understanding of motherhood and motherliness. It is especially important not to blame your behavior on your parents, and especially on your mother. For example, people say, "My mother never showed me how to do this or never gave me that. So how should I be able to do it or have it?" Look after yourself, like a good mother.

■ MOTHER-IN-LAW

The "other" or "second" mother is often taken as a symbol of all the negative and unfulfilled aspects you experienced with your own mother. The right time for necessary clarification, discussion, and common activities is when the moon is in the sign of Taurus, Libra, or especially Pisces.

■ NEIGHBORS

They are especially important and especially approachable when the moon is in Gemini.

■ PARENTAL ROLE

On the one hand, we ourselves have had parents, and, on the other hand, we are either already a parent or are preparing to become one, or we resist the idea of taking on a parental role. The reciprocal relationship between parent and child is decisive in shaping our identity as individuals and our sexual roles as women or men. This is true even in cases when at first glance the question of parenting seems to have no special role, as, for example, with a manager who seems to be married only to his career. And yet, the way he experiences this job, the way he organizes it and carries it out, is primarily determined by his identity and his understanding of roles. If we want to avoid being ruled throughout our lives by unconscious factors such as these, it is important that, at each stage of life, we address the topic of parenthood once again. The effect of the moon in the signs of Taurus, Libra, and Pisces is especially suited for this purpose.

■ PROCREATION

Sometimes it is said that with the help of the lunar calendar you could select the sex of your child, as if you were ordering it from a catalogue. According to the traditional astrological view, the signs of fire and of air—Aries, Leo, Sagittarius, Gemini, Libra, and Aquarius—are seen as male, while the signs of earth and water—Taurus, Virgo, Capricorn, Cancer, Scorpio, and Pisces—are considered female. The idea is that if impregnation occurs on a day when the moon is in a male sign, the child will be a boy, and conversely, with the moon positioned in a female sign of the zodiac, the result will be a girl. Now, it so happens that these traditional ideas about the male and the female have begun to falter. But more important, if you're not prepared to accept a child as it is and will be, you might want to think about how open you are towards a person who is not so much at your disposal.

■ PUBERTY

Puberty certainly is a characteristic of adolescence, but sometimes adolescence seems to extend into old age. Today, people seem to be maturing later, and often the transition into adulthood not only arrives late, but once it arrives, takes many years to complete. This is why nowadays symptoms of puberty such as acne, attitudes of protest, a special irritability, and problems of identity—swinging from feelings of omnipotence to those of impotence—can be found in many people far beyond the age of 18.

In the annual calendar, it is the summer solstice that stands for the initiation into adult life. The summer solstice takes place at the transition from Gemini to Cancer; and every time the moon moves from Gemini to Cancer, you are confronted again with the unresolved issues of your personal puberty. It's a good idea to understand these days as a special opportunity to find yourself and to live more consciously.

■ SCHOOL

See First Day of School

SCHOOLCHILDREN

During the first seven years of life, children are subject to the sign of Aries; during the age from 8 to 14, they are under the sign of Taurus; and from 15 to 21, under the sign of Gemini. The school years of your children are thus mostly in the signs of Taurus and Gemini. Professional training and university studies are in the sign of Gemini and/or Cancer. In order to manage these matters well and to make sure that they develop in a positive way, choose days when the moon is in the relevant sign. *See* Toddlers

SECOND BIRTH

When someone has come close to dying in an accident, some people say, "Now you have a second chance at life." How true! Yet must a small or great catastrophe occur before we can have a second chance?

Your spiritual readiness to fashion your personal life in this manner according to your own ideas and goals is most clear and strong when the moon is in the signs of Leo and Scorpio.

"After the first birth, which grounds the existence of a person, the second birth signifies the beginning of a self-chosen existence: a self-tested lifestyle, which takes the place of traditional behavior and thinking. Relations based on affinity take the place of relations based on blood (old relations, of course, can be confirmed as new relations) and one's adopted home becomes more important than one's place of birth (it is, of course, possible, but not necessary, that these two would be identical). The great and small matters of personal life are determined more through will and consciousness rather than through custom and repetition."

—Evelin Bürger and Johannes Fiebig

SENIORS

You have the best chance of finding the right appreciation of seniors when the moon is in the sign of Capricorn. An ideal time for beginning or improving a program of care is when the moon is in Virgo. The moon in the sign of Gemini will support you in finding the right mixture of intimacy and distance, of sharing and autonomy, when living together with parents and other older relatives.

SIBLINGS

Every sign of the zodiac is excellent for pleasant experiences with your siblings. If you have to confront your siblings, however, avoid the sign of Pisces and give preference to those times when the moon is in Cancer. This will make it easier to define yourself spiritually and to assert your personal autonomy.

SISTER

The sister largely determines your personal image of femininity. This is true for women as well as for men. If you don't have a sister, you might be missing something in the experience of the feminine. This lack can gradually be compensated for through female friends. To deal with all matters and occasions concerning sisters, the moon in the sign of Taurus or Cancer is especially well positioned!

STAY-AT-HOME

Some people fear the day when the last child will leave home. For this reason, they might be raising a stay-at-home. They would be wiser to concentrate instead on the tasks and opportunities of the mature phase of their own life. Every person has a calling and talents that are waiting to be used. The days when the moon is waxing in Capricorn are the right time to become clearer about, and to concentrate on, your own calling.

TODDLERS

According to a traditional astrological rule, a person enters a new stage of life every seven years. Every stage of life is assigned to a sign of the zodiac. As mentioned before, Aries is responsible for the first seven years of life. From the age of 8 to 14, it is Taurus. And in this way, every seven years another sign follows. For dealing with toddlers, therefore, the moon in Aries gives you an absolute advantage. *See* Schoolchildren

UNCLES AND AUNTS

Uncles and aunts symbolize the customs, the habits, and the taboos of your relatives. The relationship you have to these family members shows how you have dealt with the values and attitudes of your family. The moon in the sign of Virgo—in every lunar phase—is especially favorable for needed clarification, but also for celebrations and other special occasions.

WAKE

This is both the opposite and the completion of Baptism. The purpose is to say farewell to the deceased, to support the next of kin, and finally to deal with your own consternation about death and dying. The moon in the sign of Pisces will support and console you with respect to the necessary parting. For the support and help of the next of kin, *see* Friends, Neighbors, *and* Uncles and Aunts.

LOVE AND PARTNERSHIP

AGREEMENT

The right time is when the moon is in Libra.

ANNIVERSARY

A day on which love takes center stage is especially wholesome in the sign of Leo. Married couples, of course, generally celebrate their anniversary, and unmarried couples take the date of their first meeting, first date, or the first night spent together. For the significance of the different lunar signs, *see* Wedding Day.

BELIEFS ABOUT LOVE

What beliefs do you have about love? Some wish, for example, that a love relationship would require as little effort as possible or cause as little stress as possible. Then there is also the traditional concept of the partner as the "better half," in which two "opposites attract," and the two halves are supposed to make one whole. The objection to this idea is that when two half-people get together, the resulting relationship will also be a thing done by halves, with both individuals foregoing the great opportunities of their lives.

Another traditional belief about love: "Birds of a feather flock together." Here it is agreement between two people that guarantees happiness in love. But here too there are objections. If you seek a person with whom you can agree in everything, who understands you on every issue, then there is really only one person for you—yourself!

Thus, today there are more questionable than feasible beliefs about love, but that is why it's so rewarding to grapple with this issue. Beliefs about love are something like guidelines for your behavior in a partnership. The right time to occupy yourself with this topic is during the waxing moon in Libra.

BODILY CONTACT

Without bodily contact, we live like plant without food. Yet there are many levels and forms of bodily contact, from shaking hands to massages and all the way to intimate caresses. You do not necessarily have to wait until others touch and massage you. Start with yourself and then reach out to others. The best lunar times are Taurus, Virgo, and Capricorn.

CLIMAX, SEXUAL

A wedding is often considered a success when it is followed by ultimate intimate experiences. This is one of the most important and beautiful reasons for paying attention to the quality of time and finding the right point in time to recognize and make the best possible use of special opportunities in every aspect of life. Henry Miller once remarked that sexual climaxes are as good or as bad as our everyday ups and downs—as the ability we have to stimulate and invigorate ourselves in all the affairs of life. For this purpose, the moon in Leo and the days of a full moon are especially inviting.

"The sexual climax is also a parable, an example of how in every area of life we can gather all personal power and desire, concentrate, and employ it in the focal point of the moment."

—Johannes Fiebig

CRISES

These can be dangerous, but also useful. Here it is less the right timing than the right understanding that allows you to separate the wheat from the chaff. The moon in Sagittarius or the moon in Aquarius offers a good occasion for such insights.

DECLARATIONS OF LOVE

When the heart is filled with love, it is always the right time to express it. The optimal time is when the moon is in Virgo. The joy that we discover in ourselves and which we share with another is part of what makes our "long journey through a short life" so wonderful. Share, speak to strangers, and let your partner in on your secrets. Put an end to the dictum "Always criticize, praise seldom or never," or the other way around. Do not wait until your partner guesses what your needs are. Tell what they are, but also say what you are going to do for your partner. Have you ever thought of making a declaration of love to yourself? Again, the moon in Libra and also the moon in Aquarius are the right times for this purpose.

DESIRE

The right time can hardly be determined by means of a calendar. Every lunar sign and every lunar phase has its very own pleasurable qualities! In any event, don't ignore the moon in the sign of Leo!

DIVORCE

Divorces obviously cannot be avoided. While they are not always desirable, they need not bear the stigma of failure. Sometimes a divorce is a belated solution, which, after many detours, finally acknowledges the differences between two people. The more the individuality of the partners in a relationship suffers, the more necessary is a clear distinction between them. If this is neglected, then all that finally remains is the divorce as an outward distinction.When

"A wonderful life together can develop when people learn to love the distance between each other. For only then can they fully behold one another against the background of the open sky."

—Rainer Maria Rilke

the moon is in the sign of Gemini, Libra, or Pisces, it is a favorable time to make necessary distinctions and to appreciate them.

■ FANTASIES, SEXUAL

Like all fantasies and fond wishes, sexual fantasies need to be interpreted. In this way, we can take them seriously without taking them for gospel truth. Dreams and fantasies transmit a message, sometimes in a very obvious, sometimes in a more indirect, way. The right time for inquiring into the meaning of these messages is when the moon is in Scorpio, especially in the transition from Scorpio to Sagittarius.

■ FEMININITY

The best time for everything connected with this topic is the moon in Taurus. The moon in Libra and the moon in Pisces are also very effective.

■ GENDER ROLES

Your own identity as a woman or a man needs to be relived and redefined constantly. Exceptionally suitable for this purpose are the moon in Aries and the moon in Taurus, as well as the nights of a full moon.

■ GOALS OF LOVE

A typical goal of love when the moon is in Aries is that even after many years a love relationship will still be full of movement and adventure, even in the sexual domain.

The idea that love and partnership do not become less important over time, but more precious and even more pleasurable, is a goal in the sign of Taurus.

Essential to the moon in Gemini is that, even after many years, the partner will not become boring, and that humor does not diminish in the relationship.

A growing spiritual understanding coupled with affection and reliability is vital with the moon in Cancer.

For Leo, power and spiritedness are especially important. If, in the course of time, a relationship or partnership discovers and develops more and more areas in which desire and love have their place, the moon in Leo will have reached its goal of love.

In the sign of Virgo, we are dealing with the "harvest" in life: The characteristic goals of this sign are that a love relationship help the partners bring order into their lives and that the relationship bear practical fruits.

As far as Libra is concerned, love and justice describe the relevant goals of love, including justice towards one's own needs.

For Scorpios, profound passion is the highest goal (even if sometimes they try to hide it!).

For Sagittarius, great artistic skills and great desire are the best elixir of love.

The prominent goal of love in Capricorn is that love promote the career and the "calling" of each partner—and that love itself become a calling.

The prospect of combining love and freedom is what wakes the ambition of Aquarius.

And the goal of love in the sign of Pisces is to follow the great dreams of life to "the other end of the rainbow."

■ HEART-TO-HEART TALK

The best moon signs for a heart-to-heart talk are days when the moon is in Aries, because of its openness and directness, and of Libra, because of its diplomacy and ability to see two sides to every question.

■ INDEPENDENCE

When it concerns your independence in or outside the partnership, you will be supported in a special way by the moon in the signs of Aries, Virgo, and Aquarius.

■ JEALOUSY

We are very possessive when the moon is in the sign of Taurus, but we reach true jealousy in Scorpio. It is here that passionate desire, personal implacability, and anger about what is lacking or opportunities that have been missed come together! This can sometimes be a dangerous mixture. Yet, interestingly enough, in the sign of Scorpio understanding and forgiveness are also especially pronounced—and all the more are you able to love yourself and your partner.

KISSING

Happy people do not count the hours, and unhappy ones seldom kiss or kiss all the time. The moon in Taurus correlates to this difficult and/or particularly wonderful activity.

LOVE

The moon in Cancer is the best time to practice this art.

"The most important step in this regard is to learn to be able to be alone with yourself without reading, without listening to the radio, without smoking or drinking. In fact, the ability to concentrate means the same thing as the ability to be alone with oneself, and just this ability is a precondition for the ability to love. If I cling to another person because I cannot stand on my own feet, this person can perhaps be my lifesaver, but our relationship is not love. Paradoxically, the ability to be alone is the precondition for the ability to love."

—Erich Fromm, "The Art of Loving"

LOVE AFFAIR

The best times for a love affair are when the moon is in Scorpio or Sagittarius. But for love any time is the right time.

MASCULINITY

The best time for everything connected with this topic is the moon in the sign of Aries or Capricorn. Even though Capricorn traditionally counts as a feminine sign, it is very effective in this regard. According to astrological laws, Mars, the ruler of Aries, is exalted in Capricorn and is thus in its most powerful position.

MOURNING

Tears flow most abundantly under a moon in one of the water signs—Cancer, Scorpio, and Pisces. The moon in Scorpio lets you feel your grief most profoundly, but it is also helpful in working out this sorrow.

MUTUAL INTERESTS

The significance of "having things in common" in a relationship is not as clear as is often thought. Having things in common creates a spontaneous understanding and a spontaneous intimacy. However, relationships that are defined to a high degree through initial common interests may be put to a severe test when the stock of interests is used up. There is also truth in the phrase "Opposites attract." Today, most family psychologists work from the assumption that common interests are indispensable for the happiness and durability of a relationship. Here it is not primarily a matter of the quantity of time spent together or of the number of activities shared, but rather of their intensity and significance—of their quality. The moon in Gemini and the moon in Sagittarius are the right times for happy decisions.

■ OPENNESS

The optimal time for openness in love and partnership is during every full moon, and when the moon is in Pisces.

■ ROMANCE

The three water signs—Cancer, Scorpio, and Pisces—are the romantics among the signs of the zodiac. Yet earth signs—Taurus, Virgo, and Capricorn—are strongly affected by the topic of romance as well. These "sober" and "pragmatic" signs often become quite enthusiastic when they're on cloud nine. Perhaps because romance is normally neglected, these realistic characters are often surprisingly susceptible to illusions and fantasies, if these come wrapped in a sufficiently romantic package. Yet, if you learn to protect yourself against such illusions, Taurus, Virgo, and Capricorn are in a good position to offer a loving relationship a more lasting form.

■ SECRETS

Secrets in a relationship or partnership represent a necessary protection of the sphere of intimacy and the personal character of the individual. On the other hand, they can also reveal a lack of trust or of interest on the part of one of the partners. Use the moon in Gemini, or especially in Scorpio, in order to gain a more fruitful understanding of the secrets in your relationship.

SECURITY

The reliability and the naturalness that we experience in a relationship are especially shaped by the sense of security a relationship gives us. Surprisingly, however, different things give us a feeling of security at different times.

With the moon in Aries, for example, security means above all shared adventures, as well as the shared experience of mastering difficulties and special challenges, the desire to be the best in a certain field, and to set something in motion for this purpose.

With the moon in Taurus, the pleasure of the senses and sensuality are most prominent, and also the achievement of certain results.

With the moon in Gemini, however, a delightful security is created through conversation and the exchange of ideas, news, and spiritual experiences.

With the moon in Cancer, it is the independence—the integrity of the individual—that offers security—and also endless cuddling.

With the moon in Leo, we feel most protected when our self-will is in full bloom. *See* Self-Will

With the moon in Virgo, we feel secure when we are devoting ourselves to a task or service, and when we feel appreciated.

With a moon in Libra, security is on one hand bound up with personal prestige and recognition, and, on the other hand, with justice.

With the moon in Scorpio, we feel protected when we get what we want.

Large projects, distant travels, and idealistic goals offer security when the moon is in Sagittarius.

When the moon is in Capricorn, security means either standing alone and unreachable on a pedestal, or feeling existentially completely connected and intimate with someone.

With the moon in Aquarius, we feel secure when we have some distance between ourselves and our partner and can observe ourselves with detachment.

Under a moon in Pisces, we feel safe and secure when we have goals and principles on which we can wholeheartedly depend and to which we can completely dedicate our human existence.

■ SEDUCTION

Each one of the twelve lunar signs has its own art of seduction—and when needed, of course, its own defense mechanisms against unwanted attempts at seduction.

You are especially attractive, charming, and convincing at times when the moon is in your personal lunar sign (see tables on pages 127 to 129).

■ SELF-WILL

A relationship is successful to the extent that each of the participants is able to grow in it. Hence, properly understood, self-will is less a problem than a necessary condition for a happy partnership.

"There is one virtue which I love dearly, a single one. It is called self-will.... All other virtues that are loved and praised so much are obedience to laws given by human beings. It is only self-will that does not respect these laws. The person who is self-willed obeys a different law, one that is unconditionally sacred: the 'will' or 'sense' of one's 'self'."

—Hermann Hesse

Disputes, rivalries, and jealousy in a relationship are always positive and productive if they contribute towards questioning unbroken self-will and bringing out a true sense of self. As is the case with health, self-will is not everything, but without it everything else would be experienced as empty and senseless. The best time for the virtue of self-will is the moon in Cancer, and also the moon in Virgo.

■ SEX LIFE

Every lunar phase and every lunar sign shape our sex lives. It is a reflection of our vivacity, our intensity, and the secrets of our lives. Especially useful lunar phases are the full moon and the new moon, as well as days and nights that vary from individual to individual and can be recognized by the fact that you are very moody or "willful." Men and women both have their periods. During these times, you are particularly close to your drives and instincts.

SPACE

The moon in Gemini and the moon in Sagittarius affect the right measure of distance and closeness in your partnership, especially when the moon shifts from the ascending to the descending direction—or back again.

TENDERNESS

The right time for tenderness is when the need is great and the external obstacles are small. Surprisingly, every lunar sign has its own qualities in this regard.

WEDDINGS

Here the moon in Gemini is ideal. According to ancient tradition, two lovers "know" each other on their wedding day. This combination of love and knowledge is best expressed by the twin symbolism of the Gemini.

WEDDING DAYS

Using the lunar tables you can calculate in what sign the moon was on your wedding day, and in the lunar calendar (starting at page 132), you can see in which sign the moon will be on this year's wedding anniversary. (People who are not married, or who do not wish to get married, can substitute any date that is meaningful to them.)

A wedding day with the moon in Aries suggests a stormy love life.

A wedding moon in Taurus stands for sensual and productive times.

The moon in Gemini on your wedding day promises a high point in love and knowledge.

The moon in Cancer on a wedding day indicates deep feelings, which can speak to many secluded sides of the soul.

The moon in Leo on a wedding day tells of self-confirmation and sexual satisfaction.

The moon in Virgo on a wedding day indicates self-confidence and independence.

The moon in Libra on a wedding day promises gratification even of vague and extravagant needs.

The moon in Scorpio on a wedding day signals spiritual longing and great respect in love.

The moon in Sagittarius on a wedding day emphasizes yearning and an appetite for new adventures.

The moon in Capricorn on a wedding day stands for completely unknown possibilities of happiness, because new talents are surfacing and old disputes can be settled.

The moon in Aquarius on a wedding day signifies a new and rich measure of individual freedom, of humor, and of spirit.

The moon in Pisces on this special day promises a wonderful and far-reaching fulfillment of spiritual needs and desires.

■ WITHDRAWAL

The right time is the new moon. Yes and No are the two poles—even in love—without which there is no suspense, no energy. One pole would be quite meaningless without the other. *See* Space

ADVENTURES AND CHALLENGES

■ ADVENTURE

The optimal time for adventures is the waxing moon in Aries as well as the waning moon in Sagittarius.

"Adventures and peak experiences represent turning points in our lives that are not always and not only pleasant.... Ecstatic and apparently magical experiences... take place in our everyday lives."

—Klausbernd Vollmar

■ AGE, OLD

Old age is one of the greatest adventures a human being can have if he or she is in fairly good health. An important precondition is having goals in life that accompany your development, and with which you grow. The goals you set for yourself must not be unattainable, but they should not be so insignificant as to provide no incentive. The best tasks of life are characterized by the fact that they mobilize all your powers. If you don't have such tasks, the first step consists of searching for them. The waxing and waning moon in Sagittarius, especially in its transition to Capricorn, will help you in your search.

■ BAD NEWS

If we manage not to lose our heads every time we hear bad news, this allows us to expand our horizons by working through even unpleasant and unwelcome truths. In this way you can contribute towards realizing more light, warmth, and humanity. This is not always easy! The best time for this is when the moon is in Gemini. The new moon as well can support you in your efforts.

> ***"The purpose of enlightenment is to be able to gaze into the darkness with a clear eye."***
>
> —Nikos Kazantzakis

■ BEAUTY

For many this is also an important goal in life. As with charisma, there is beauty according to society, a standard that is and remains impersonal and replaceable. But there is also a true and personal beauty. In spite of the multiplicity of ideals and ideas of beauty, true beauty is generally made up of an agreement between inner attitude, personal composure, and outward appearance and mannerisms. It is an expression of the true form a human being embodies. In this regard, you are supported by the lunar power in the sign of Taurus and Libra.

■ BEGINNING A CAREER

Capricorn and Aries are the signs that offer you optimal support.

■ BEST, THE

It can be an honorable ambition to want to be the best. An eternal dissatisfaction with yourself, though, can have the result that the good is never felt to be sufficient and that only the best is worth striving for. We are especially sensitive to this dissatisfaction when the moon is in Libra. Yet this is also where the solutions to these questions and problems lie.

■ CHARISMA

The desire for charisma expresses the need for recognition and attention. As psychologists have discovered, perfect manners, a radiant appearance, and other pleasant characteristics often reveal a certain aversion to conflict and contradiction. In such a case, we are dealing with an exaggerated fear of "getting into hot water." But there is also a personal charisma that is convincing and has an immediate effect on others. It is based—this too has been discovered by psychologists—on the fact that you have granted yourself important wishes and have managed to overcome essential fears. As a result, a natural charisma arises that can also consist of external features, but does not depend on them. This charisma is based on personal clarity. The right time to polish this is when the moon is in Aquarius!

■ CLEVERNESS

To have "know-how" is to have a practical cleverness that counts among the great adventures and challenges, because here you experience how to attain or bring about what you want. This cleverness thrives on observation and expertise. Here, the right moon sign is Virgo.

■ DESIRE

Desire, craving, longing—these are connected with highly concentrated spiritual wishes and personal needs. It is possible to be truly fixated on a certain goal. This is not necessarily negative. It can be, for example, an essential precondition for holding on to important aspirations even when there is enormous resistance. You simply need to discover what the needs that are so dear to your heart mean for you in the end. Then, even the greatest challenge or the most "unrealistic" vision might be a task that you would master with flair and skill if you could just hold on long enough. In another case, however, even the smallest temptation or the most promising prospects could be hazardous. It is a matter of walking a delicate line, which you could surely master if you took your needs seriously—interpreting them like dreams, and above all living them. Try to understand the significance of what moves you. The right time for this purpose is always the moon in Scorpio.

ENDING A CAREER

The moon in Libra or in Capricorn indicates the optimal periods for all related activity.

FAME

This goal is one for which many people are prepared to sacrifice a lot. Even nowadays it seems that people quite often make the same deal as Faust, who sold his soul to the devil in order to fulfill such dreams. Andy Warhol said, "What counts in fame is its content. Without personal content you may be famous, but you are also exchangeable." In this respect, the moon in Gemini or in Virgo is critical. The moon in Sagittarius, on the other hand, is best.

FAMILY FUN

Life in a larger group—family, roommates, or other teams and life partnerships—counts, among the great adventures and challenges, just as much as, for example, success in a career or the fulfillment of your fondest dreams. Formulate your goals when the moon is in Pisces, plan them with the moon in Taurus, check them with the moon in Virgo, and realize them when the moon is in Sagittarius! The joy will be all yours.

FIRST, THE

Like the desire to be the best, or to shine with your uniqueness, the need to be the first in some area may also be merely a fixation or a whim. The deeds of a pioneer, on the other hand, are something else. From time to time, every person inevitably enters new territory. Many regulations, agreements, and customs just cannot be taken over from models or examples, but must be personally discovered and developed. The thought of being the first can spur you on. Your spiritual openness will be greatest for this purpose when the moon is in Aries. *See* The Best

FREEDOM

Freedom—in the sense of independence—is especially emphasized by the moon in Aquarius. And freedom from fear and desire—the art of being happy without desire—is influenced by the moon in Scorpio.

GOODBYES

Coming and going at the appropriate time is handled especially well when the moon is in Virgo. It is an art to be able to handle a necessary departure—whether it be in our private lives or in our careers—as a "power exit" and a dignified ending. The right time for this purpose is when the moon is in Scorpio (preferably the waning moon).

HAPPINESS

"Happiness means that we manage to make something happen. We carry certain desires within us that are too crucial to be allowed to disappear. And everyone probably has certain fears that are too pressing to carry around forever. A decisive element of happiness is to fulfill or take care of these essential desires and fears."

—Evelin Bürger and Johannes Fiebig

This is true for all of us, even though the content of the desires and fears can vary greatly from individual to individual. Your optimal companion on this "path of desire" is the moon in Sagittarius.

But the phases of the full moon often represent storm centers. Many desires still unfulfilled and fears still unabated are washed up on the shore. Try to accept these agitations at the time of a full moon, because in the end they will ease and shorten your path to happiness.

HEALTH

For many people, health represents Goal Number 1, even before a long life *(see* Age*)* and all other great desires, and to that extent it represents the ultimate challenge. In this book, a special section, "Health and Well-Being," has been dedicated to the topic of health. Generally, the right time for health care is when the moon is in Virgo.

HOME OF YOUR OWN

For this to be or remain a positive adventure, pay special attention to your fears and desires in connection with your housing situation when the moon is in Cancer.

HOUSEWARMING PARTY

The moon in Taurus, especially the waxing moon, is ideal for a housewarming.

INDIVIDUALITY

This is one of the great goals and challenges of life. The right time is the waxing or waning moon in Aquarius. *See* Uniqueness

LOVE

The section on "Love and Partnership" in this book is dedicated to this great adventure. Here is a pleading for mature love that is not afraid to go a long way.

"The person who does not know anything does not love anything. The person who cannot do anything does not understand anything....But the person who understands also loves, notices, and sees....He who thinks that all fruits ripen at the same time as the strawberries does not know about grapes."

—Paracelsus

Generally, a favorable time in matters of love is when the moon is in Gemini or Libra.

MAGIC

Every human being has something totally unique. If you invest in your individuality and live it to the fullest, you will accomplish exceptional things. This sounds like a miracle, and it is miraculous, but we are not

"All the wonderful and magical experiences you have made and will make in your life also concern the magic of individuality. Thus, for example, the magic of love or the magic of falling in love are experiences that imply that you have found your character and that your personal uniqueness is confirmed."

—Evelin Bürger and Johannes Fiebig

dealing with witchcraft, but with the wholly natural application of living and growing individuality. Thus, if you want to create magic and enchantment, you need to draw upon the experience of your individual course and style of life. You will find optimal phases of power and the right time with the moon in the sign of Gemini or Virgo.

■ MID-LIFE CRISIS

One of the more sensational studies of the change of lifestyle in the industrialized countries concluded that the so-called mid-life crisis is no longer limited to the age from the mid-thirties to the mid-forties. Between the age of puberty and the age of retirement, no age group is immune to a great personal crisis. This has even changed the effects of the years of menopause in women. For each age, therefore, it is a matter of finding your own center. The moon in Leo and the moon in Capricorn are the right advisors for this purpose.

■ PARTNERSHIPS

Love is not only the suitable standard for measuring a close relationship between two people. Even in the relationship that you have with yourself, as well as in all day-to-day contacts and encounters, love is, strictly speaking, the most sensible criterion. Love is not just a feeling, but also a precondition for the optimal advancement of many needs and talents! The moon in Libra supports you.

■ PROMOTION

Not for everyone, but for some, this can be one of the high points of life! You will experience clear empowerment when the moon is in Taurus or in Capricorn. The moon in Leo or Sagittarius is not without benefits either, but with the moon in a fire sign be sure you don't overdo your efforts!

■ RECOGNITION

Not for all, but for many people, the experience of wide and unanimous recognition is extremely important. At the appropriate time, fair and unprejudiced recognition—praise, congratulation, confirmation, or response—can work wonders and be an antidote to an unhealthy egotism. In general, the right time for this purpose is the moon in Libra.

■ SATISFACTION

On many occasions we have the feeling that we have not received enough, that we have been shortchanged or haven't gotten what we deserved. In light of this, the urge to have enough, and to experience satisfaction, is a legitimate and understandable desire that we carry within us. As long as this satisfaction is lacking, we feel treated unjustly by life. The right time to heal this flaw is when the moon is in Libra.

■ SENSATIONAL NEWS

The desire for sensational news is based on the attraction of the unusual. In practical terms, however, this means that you are searching for a daily life with less routine and more realized dreams and true sensations. The right time to pursue these interests is when the moon is in Aquarius.

■ STRESS

Stress is necessary for the activation of all our vital powers. Only after we have passed a few positive tests are we able to distinguish a healthy or productive investment of energy from truly unhealthy stress, and then avoid the unhealthy kind. All three fire signs—Aries, Leo, and Sagittarius—are involved in this. The waxing moon in Leo is most effective.

■ SUCCESS

The moon in Taurus or Sagittarius (especially the moon in Sagittarius) is the ideal godfather here.

■ TIME

For many people the idea of finally having enough time for yourself seems the pinnacle of happiness and what can be achieved in this life. For this purpose, the right sign to turn to is Aquarius. When the moon is in this sign, it is time to look into the mirror, to accept yourself, and thus to accept your own time.

■ TRAVEL

Besides vacations, adventures, and recreation, a major trip also signifies the need to make more of your life, to expand your horizons. The moon in Sagittarius will support you in this, in an exceptional way.

UNEMPLOYMENT

This is usually a low point of personal experience—at least, it seems that way at first. Like any crisis, however, unemployment represents both a danger and an opportunity. The opportunity lies in the opening of new doors for you, and in your being more likely to take advantage of them in the future, thereby achieving more. Also, this unemployment could result in your coming to understand that career and worldly success are not everything. So, as you see, opposite conclusions may be drawn from the existing situation. Nothing will help you more in this area than the moon in Cancer or in Capricorn.

UNIQUENESS

The highest dream for some people would be to own a monopoly. You would be the only one, important and indispensable to all. In the economy as well as in love, however, monopolies are not necessarily the most healthy thing. And it does not seem very promising to try to attach your uniqueness to something like this. We all have certain talents—gifts, skills, and callings—which define us in individual ways. The most realistic and sensible method of underscoring your personal uniqueness seems to be to discover these talents and use them. The lunar phase that will help you especially in this is the full moon. And the one sign that is just right for these endeavors: Capricorn!

WEALTH

Your existence and your individuality are your greatest assets. The question of how you maintain and invest in this world, and what is special to you, is of utmost importance. Nowhere will you see your personal strengths and weaknesses in connection with inward and outward wealth as clearly as with the moon in Virgo.

WISH FULFILLMENT

See Desire *and* Happiness

The moon in Sagittarius is decisive here.

WORRIES

As long as we believe the alternatives of good and bad still exist, we will continue to be worried about reaching the good and avoiding the bad. The person who lives without worries is "beyond good and evil," which is a theological concept of heaven or hell. In other words: Living without worries could mean hell on earth because you do not care, and act without conscience or scruples. Or, living without worries can also be heaven on earth, if you have made your peace with God and the world. The moon in Virgo and the moon in Pisces will help you here.

HOME AND DAILY LIFE

AIRING THE HOUSE

An air day—Gemini, Libra, Aquarius—with a waning moon is the best time.

ART

Your artistic ambitions grow, flourish, and thrive when the moon is in the sign of Sagittarius or Pisces.

BOOKS

The best times for dealing with literature are in the three air signs—Gemini, Libra, and Aquarius. When the moon is in Aquarius, you will have the right overview. The moon in Libra makes it easy for you to read between the lines and to understand the meaning of what is written. The moon in Gemini speeds up the processing of large amounts of data.

BOWLING

Ideal when the moon is in Capricorn.

CAR CARE

The best time is when the moon is in Cancer.

CAR REPAIR

The moon in Gemini or in Virgo is ideal.

CINEMA

See Movies

CLEANING

The right time for cleaning is when the waning moon is in Virgo.

CLOTHES

See Fashion

COOKING

The moon in Taurus and the moon in Sagittarius are the best helpers in the kitchen, for the activity author/psychologist Klausbernd Vollmar calls "daily and applied alchemy."

CYCLING

The right time is during the waning moon in Gemini.

DANCE CLUBS

Favorable times are when the moon is in Gemini or Sagittarius.

DANCING

The moon in Libra and the moon in the transition from Aries to Taurus are the best times for the art and joy of dancing.

DIARY

Writing in your diary is especially good when the moon is in Gemini.

DREAMING

In the signs of Libra and Pisces, lunar power is most likely to transform into "dream power." Fantasies, daydreams, and recollections of nightly dreams come very easily at these times. Sometimes they come all too easily, which means that you could be more at home in your dreams than in reality.

DRIVING

The optimal time for this activity is when the moon is in Cancer.

FASHION

There is an optimal time if you want to buy new clothes: the waxing moon in your personal lunar sign (you can easily determine it with the help of the tables on pages 127 to 129). Let us assume, for example, that your personal lunar sign is Libra: You will without problems hit upon the right style and put together your outfit in such a way that you will be satisfied with it in every respect when the moon is in Libra. With a waxing moon in your personal lunar sign you will shop most effectively; you will know what you want and you will have a sure sense of taste. With a waning moon in your personal sign, you will also part safely and effectively with articles of clothing that no longer suit you. Generally favorable for all questions of fashion, personal style, and taste is the sign of Cancer. All other signs (aside from your personal lunar sign) are less suitable.

■ FITNESS

There are many suitable times—always when the moon is in a fire sign—Aries, Leo, Sagittarius, for example—or in one of the earth signs—Taurus, Virgo, or Capricorn. In any of these signs, the moon will help you to become especially fit.

■ HANDBALL

All ball games played by hand—handball, volleyball, basketball, and so on—work best when the moon is in the sign of Gemini.

■ HIKING

There is no question but that the right time is when the moon is in Capricorn.

■ HOME FURNISHING

The right times for new ideas and for realizing them are the waning moon in Taurus and the waxing moon in Virgo.

■ HORSEBACK RIDING

The best time is the waning moon in Sagittarius.

■ HOUSEHOLD CHORES

Almost all household chores can be carried out more easily and effectively when the moon is waning. Generally, the days of Virgo are ideal.

■ HOUSEHOLD PLANNING

The right time is the moon in Virgo, waxing as well as waning.

■ JOGGING/RUNNING

Works best with the moon in Gemini.

■ LATEST CRAZE, THE

You will recognize it most quickly when the moon is in Gemini. During this phase you are also most able to distinguish between a "flash in the pan" and a novelty of lasting value. Pay special attention whenever the moon is in the sign of your sun (the sign under which you celebrate your birthday). Let us assume, for example, that you were born on December 30 when the sun was in the sign of Capricorn and the moon was passing through the sign of Libra. Whenever the moon is also in Capricorn, you run the danger of "forgetting" your personal moon (Libra), because the Capricorn vibration is so strong. This means that whenever the moon is in Capricorn, your Libra characteristics—true style and personal taste—will be weakened.

Every day you dress according to your mood, personal situation, and needs. But think about how fascinating it would be to adjust your personal appearance to the rhythms of the moon. You will be surprised at the variety of forms of expression you will discover for yourself. You can play with seemingly unfamiliar characteristics. At the same time you will experience very clearly the qualities of the individual signs of the zodiac which, of course, represent all the possible talents of every one of us. The table on page 85 may give you some ideas.

■ LAUNDRY

Optimal during a waning moon, especially when in a water sign—Cancer, Scorpio, or Pisces—preferably during Pisces.

■ LETTER WRITING

The moon in Gemini is ideal for writing (and receiving) letters.

■ MOVIES

Going to the movies when the moon is in the sign of Sagittarius is twice as much fun.

Qualities of the Signs

Sign of the zodiac	Definition	Color	Types
Aries	I am	red	tiger, cat, "big cats," pioneer, astronaut
Taurus	I have	brown, earth tones	country house decorator, farmer, livestock breeder, banker
Gemini	I think	light, oscillating, and iridescent colors	city life, reporter, perfumer, the latest craze
Cancer	I feel	green and blue tones, pink	self-directed, individual style
Leo	I will	orange, strong colors	manager
Virgo	I analyze	pastels, khaki, blackberry	gardener, butler, teacher
Libra	I balance	violet, gray, bright red, burgundy	pilot, attorney, umpire, judge, "The Phantom of the Opera"
Scorpio	I desire	black, white, crimson	"The Rocky Horror Picture Show"
Sagittarius	I perceive	strong, shining blue, traffic-signal red	moviegoer, entertainer
Capricorn	I use	black, brown, green	pyramid explorer, forest ranger, grave digger, gold prospector
Aquarius	I know	loud, shrill and iridescent colors	researcher, "Starlight Express," Robinson Crusoe
Pisces	I believe	sea green, rainbow colors	pastor, physician, vamp, lover

■ MUSIC
Music goes especially well when the moon is in Taurus or in Libra!

■ PARTIES
The moon in Gemini, Leo, or Libra will ensure the right party atmosphere and a great success.

■ REPAIRS
Days when the moon is in Gemini are most appropriate, because of the desire of this sign to find out how things work. Also when the moon is in Aries or Taurus, because of the ability of these signs to make a virtue out of necessity.

■ SECONDHAND ARTICLES
You will sell them most successfully with a waning moon in Taurus. With a waxing moon in Taurus, you will make the best buys.

■ SEWING
You are best served with the moon in Virgo or in Gemini: no sign is better suited for needlework.

■ SHOE CARE
Especially effective during a waning moon.

■ SHOPPING
The right time is when the moon is in Taurus.

■ SKATING
Whether rollerblading, roller-skating, or ice-skating, no time is better suited than when the moon is in Aquarius.

■ SOCCER
The moon should be in Leo or Aries, if you really want to get the ball rolling.

■ SPORTS
See Bowling, Handball, Horseback Riding, Jogging, Running, Skating, Soccer, Swimming, Tennis

■ SWIMMING

The optimal time is when the moon is in Pisces.

■ TAROT

Having tarot cards read constitutes an encounter with so-called chance and a play of intuition and profound meaning. For this purpose, your birthday, New Year's Eve, days of the full moon or the new moon, and the moon in Sagittarius are best.

■ TENNIS

Optimal during a moon in Gemini or Sagittarius.

■ TIDYING UP

The best time is when the moon is in Virgo, just before the new moon.

■ TIME MANAGEMENT

This works best with a waning moon in Aquarius, because Aquarius has the best understanding of the rhythm in which you and your environment are moving.

■ VISITS

Visiting the neighbors is best done when the moon is in Gemini. Siblings are best visited during a moon in Cancer, parents in the sign of Taurus, and aunts and uncles, as well as other relatives, in the sign of Virgo. Visits to unknown places, new locations, and so on, will go well when the moon is in Aquarius.

■ WORKING OUT

The best time is the waxing moon in Taurus.

■ YOGA

The waning moon in Virgo is especially favorable.

THE LUNAR SIGNS AND THEIR SIGNIFICANCE

Moon in Aries

Definition:	Aries—I am
Element:	Fire
Lunar phases:	Waxing moon from October until April, waning moon from April until October
Direction:	Ascending lunar power
Energy:	Heat
Food:	Protein
Nature:	Fruits

HEALTH

The head, the brain, and the face are assigned to Aries. The eyes, of course, are part of this as well, but they play a more significant role in the sign of Leo or Sagittarius. The forehead and the nose, on the other hand, are definitely Aries. The teeth are assigned to Taurus, but they are influenced by Aries and Capricorn, too. In a positive sense, Aries is the pioneer who will not give up even in the face of great difficulties. In a rather unpleasant sense, Aries represents the ram who behaves like a "bull in a china shop." Its combative and martial nature, however, represents only one side of its character. People often suppose that will is the main feature of Aries, but will belongs to Leo. Aries says: "I am," and therefore you will find optimal support from Aries when it comes to making your own existence productive and maintaining it that way.

Health problems arise during a moon in Aries when head and feet—being and consciousness—are too far from each other. The ensuing one-sidedness and half measures are detrimental to the fiery Aries. When its fire is supplied with new fuel, however, it has the surprising ability to neutralize conflict and heal illnesses—including typical head ailments such as colds, headaches, or migraines.

NATURE

When the moon is in Aries, sow and plant everything you want to have grow quickly. The moon in Aries is a good time for grafting fruit trees. Fruits do very well at this time. You may fertilize fruit, vegetables, and grain under this sign, but only during the months from April until September. Good days for pruning fruit trees and shrubs are during the waning moon in Aries.

FINANCES

The moon in Aries is the best time for starting new projects and enterprises. Your self-assertiveness, your working morale, and your loyalty towards yourself will support you in your career. Aries is able to get things moving. Pay attention to your goals!

FAMILY

If family life has adventures and challenges in store for you, you will feel absolutely comfortable at home during a moon in Aries. This is also a favorable (and sometimes necessary) time for dealing with your own experiences and ideas of masculinity and the father role.

LOVE

While the moon is in Aries, you may risk (and expect of others) more directness and spontaneity than at other times. Here it is often difficult to see the world through someone else's eyes. To put it in a positive way: This is a good time to remind yourself of your own views—even in your relationships.

ADVENTURE

The greatest challenge and the greatest reward in this sign is to be your own boss, or to be first or the leader in a certain field. All activities that serve these goals make our hearts beat faster during a moon in Aries.

AT HOME

This is a favorable time for sports, games, and excitement—a lunar period that fosters the independence of every member of the family.

THE FULL MOON IN ARIES

Danger: Feelings of omnipotence and arrogance.

Opportunity: Clear-sighted estimation of your own situation and tasks. Head and feet, being and consciousness, combine to form a conscious existence and a sovereign art of living.

THE NEW MOON IN ARIES

Danger: Feelings of powerlessness and insignificance, rage, anger.

Opportunity: Courageous step into new spiritual territory. Don't wait—start!

Moon in Taurus

Definition:	Taurus—I have
Element:	Earth
Lunar phases:	Waxing moon from November until May, waning moon from May until November
Direction:	Ascending lunar power
Energy:	Cold/rest
Food:	Salt
Nature:	Roots

HEALTH

Throat and neck, certainly, but also mouth, teeth, and ears are assigned to the sign of Taurus. Everything that comes out of the mouth is affected: speech, voice, songs, moans, sighs, and so on. In addition, Taurus relates to everything we take in through the mouth, everything we chew on and swallow. The famous "frog in the throat" deserves to be mentioned here, as well as the glutton who "bites off more than he can chew," and the one who has "had his fill."

This means that, with the moon in Taurus, health and well-being depend on the interplay of inside and outside. If, for example, your outward behavior does not agree with your inner feelings and needs, the result will be ailments and illnesses, especially in the area of the mouth and the throat.

Every kind of property (the defining phrase of this sign is "I have") brings us luck, if it fits in with our needs and demands. Something similar is true of sensuality, which is especially affected in the sign of Taurus. So, we can say that those material gains and those bodily experiences, including sexuality, that correspond exactly to our inner feelings have an absolutely wholesome and salutary effect on us. Too much or too little of something, on the other hand, might be harmful.

With typical Taurus problems, such as hoarseness, infections of the throat, the tonsils, or the pharynx, it is important to bring the relationship between inner needs and outward actions back into balance. Through the ears and the organs of equilibrium, Taurus is also concerned with maintaining personal balance and avoiding dizziness! You will find further information on this issue on pages 107–110 with the lunar sign of Libra, which also deals with balance.

NATURE

The best time to seed or plant trees, shrubs, hedges, or root vegetables is while the moon is in Taurus. Everything that grows slowly and is meant to last is good to start during this time. Whatever you harvest is well suited for preservation and storage. This is also a favorable time for controlling pests that live underground.

FINANCES

Some experts see Taurus as the financial genius of the zodiac. Basically, this assessment is justified, even though other signs, such as Virgo and Aquarius, have demonstrated special powers as well. It is a typical feature of Taurus that it can move great masses; the question is, to what purpose? You need to make sure that material wealth (possessions) and spiritual wealth (love and fulfillment) remain in harmony. Then you will achieve results under this sign of the moon that are truly worthwhile.

FAMILY

The moon in Taurus is the right time for pampering the family and the household. It is a good time to build or arrange something together. Physical contact is especially important in this phase. At the same time, it is a good opportunity to increase your independence from teachers and educators by taking teaching and learning into your own hands! Finally, the moon in Taurus also is the right time to deal with your ideas of femininity, your experiences, and your role as a mother.

LOVE

This is a sensual and erotic time (in bed as well as elsewhere). Now you and your partner have a special chance to find things in common that can enrich your life together sexually and on all other levels. The pivotal point is again clarity about one's personal needs. This also ensures that possessive jealousy and fears of loss do not become too powerful.

ADVENTURE

If sense and the senses can develop in an optimal way, you will live at the pinnacle of happiness when the moon is in Taurus—working to make money and spending money for enjoyment. The moon in Taurus, however, stands for the unity of work and enjoyment, everyday life and adventure.

AT HOME

This is the time for tidying up, for stocking up on things, for beautification, and for enjoyment. It is the right time for body care, for sleeping in, for delicious and healthy food, and for relaxing massages and self-massages.

THE FULL MOON IN TAURUS

Danger: Repression is the real problem. The full moon in Taurus is sometimes like a madhouse. You feel surprised and overtaxed by developments and encounters.

Opportunity: It consists in the realization that nothing needs to be repressed anymore. Of course, it can be unpleasant when problems are right out on the table, but these problems will no longer have hidden effects on your life. Comprehensive solutions become possible, and they offer a freedom and satisfaction previously thought impossible!

THE NEW MOON IN TAURUS

Danger: The burdens of daily life can cause especially long-lasting stress and great difficulties.

Opportunity: In this phase, absolute concentration on the daily necessities has a positive effect. Free yourself from dependencies. Freely do what is necessary.

Moon in Gemini

Definition:	Gemini—I think
Element:	Air
Lunar phases:	Waxing moon from December until June, waning moon from June until December
Direction:	Change from ascending to descending power
Energy:	Air/light
Food:	Fat
Nature:	Flowers

HEALTH

The shoulders, arms, and hands, as well as the lungs together with the bronchial tubes, are assigned to Gemini. The hands deal with what we take on and really carry out, but also with what we grasp. The key phrase of Gemini is: "I think." This concerns the cerebral work of thinking and of intellectual work. Therefore, the health and well-being of Gemini depend especially on how well head and hand—or theory and practice—agree.

The lungs are concerned with breathing, the supply of oxygen, and the exchange between yourself and the environment. Here the breath becomes a mirror for the right connection between thinking and doing, between yourself and the rest of the world. With the moon in Gemini, it is especially important to work on this interaction in order to protect your health. Breathing exercises and gymnastics for the hands, arms, and shoulders are especially recommended, as are psychological observations, without which the necessary understanding would not be possible.

NATURE

This is the time to sow, plant, and cultivate the climbers. The time is also right for planting and cultivating flowers and flowering plants, using cautious fertilization for the purpose of increased blooms. If possible, avoid watering indoor plants at this time.

FINANCES

The moon in Gemini is the right time for business deals and negotiations. It is also an ideal time for brainstorming, as well as for the art of thinking through new ideas and considering their consequences. Just don't forget that ideas, thoughts, discussions, and contacts should lead to definite results.

FAMILY

This is an appropriate time for a heart-to-heart talk, for family conferences, for the exchange of news and gossip. It is possible to neutralize tensions if, besides exchanging information, you also truly try to understand the other person. The moon in Gemini is the right time to deal with your parents and with the role of a parent.

LOVE

The "chemistry" of a relationship proves its value when the moon is in Gemini. Bring variety into your relationship and engage in spontaneous and witty ideas. Speak what is on your mind.

ADVENTURE

With the moon in Gemini, it is a great celebration and an adventure to travel light and be free to give yourself over to new ideas, inspirations, and impressions. Necessities and duties need not be ignored, but should be dealt with and taken care of in such a way that a balance between play and seriousness is achieved.

AT HOME

The moon in Gemini is the right time for all small repairs in the house, as well as for visits to the neighbors.

THE FULL MOON IN GEMINI

Danger: Impulsive reactions can lead to inappropriate actions. Here there is the danger that "One hand does not know what the other is doing."

Opportunity: It consists in finding yourself and being able to live very consciously on many levels at once. It means being carefree through a conscious proximity to "God," which is achieved because you have mastered and removed problems.

THE NEW MOON IN GEMINI

Danger: There is a danger of thoughtlessness and mental blackout. Yet the opposite danger lurks as well: a mental overexcitement, but with physical paralysis or motionlessness. Here it is important to examine yourself and to put your trust in a higher power. Good breathing will see you through the difficulties.

Opportunity: The conscious experience of farewells and new beginnings. You need, so to speak, to stop and turn off the computer, and then start a new program.

Moon in Cancer

Definition:	Cancer—I feel
Element:	Water
Lunar phases:	Waxing moon from January until July, waning moon from July until January
Direction:	Descending lunar power
Energy:	Water
Food:	Carbohydrates
Nature:	Leaves

HEALTH

The chest, breasts, abdomen, and stomach are assigned to the sign of Cancer. In the sequence of the signs of the zodiac from Aries to Pisces, Cancer is the first in which the moon has a descending direction of action. With this it also becomes clear that here we are dealing with inner powers and with the inner life. This concerns processes that are not always easy to grasp. Your feelings are very important for your health and well-being when the moon is in Cancer. At the same time, it is this sign that most clearly experiences contradictions and oppositions in the area of feeling. For feelings are not exclusively positive and exclusively helpful just because they are feelings. Unfortunately, this is often forgotten when feelings are praised one-sidedly: "Listen to your feelings." Certainly, where hitherto the intellect has ruled, it is important for balance to put a general emphasis on the power of the soul and of feelings. But then you need to look more closely and make distinctions. There are pleasant and unpleasant, meaningful and meaningless feelings. There are important and unimportant desires, justified and unjustified fears. While the moon is in Gemini, we experience the notorious "two souls in one chest." The purpose of the exercise is to learn to distinguish and understand our own feelings. What is pleasant or unpleasant, good or bad—for ourselves or for others—is not written in stone for all time, but needs to be determined again and again. There is a saying that "everything is in flux." But only if we constantly deal with our own feelings and the feelings of others does our spiritual life remain in flux. The polarity between sympathy and antipathy, between desires and fears, and so on, generates the tension—the slope—which allows the water to flow.

NATURE

The moon in Cancer is the right time for planting and cultivating leafy vegetables, and also for controlling pests that live above the ground. Now is a good time to mow the lawn (preferably during a waxing moon), water your indoor plants, and fertilize your flowers.

FINANCES

With the moon in the sign of Cancer, you are concentrating completely on your soul and your feelings. But it is just this familiarity in dealing with inner needs and motives that gives you a skilled hand in dealing with business partners, colleagues at work, and so on. At the same time, we sense a pronounced need for material security, for a protective framework in which we are able to experience and live our feelings to the fullest. In this way we develop the ability and the readiness to make really worthwhile business deals and achieve corresponding results. Today, meditation and market research no longer preclude each other at all. This is the optimal time for good business deals, that is, "win-win" deals that truly benefit everyone involved.

FAMILY

Generally speaking, this is a good—even a very good—time for family life. The reservations refer only to the fact that occasionally the striving for outward, material security becomes so great in this sign that family life suffers as a consequence. Or it may be that your own feelings seem to find so little resonance in the "bad outside world" that the family becomes a substitute for the fulfillment of your desires and for competence in all areas of life. The biggest weak point here is a helplessness in dealing with feelings, which is usually the result of ignorance. Make your own experiences, encourage other family members to make their own experiences, and you will have a stimulating family life. This is also the right time to deal with the role of a sibling.

LOVE

A suitable or even necessary time for re-experiencing and reshaping closeness and distance, limitations, and openness, in a partnership. Here it is a matter of preventing, as much as possible, becoming stuck in certain roles, so that the encounter from person to person, and from heart to heart, becomes and remains possible.

ADVENTURE

When the moon is in Cancer, it's a good idea to spend some time with yourself, to go out into nature, to find your roots, to meditate, and to dream. At the same time, in this sign we are enticed and lured by exotic and precious objects and goals. A distant country, a foreign religion or way of life, a fascinating person may now call to be visited or experienced. Grant yourself this adventure.

AT HOME

Cutting hair is not recommended at this time. Doing the laundry and cleaning, however, are appropriate. It is also a good time to clear up problems and conflicts. And it is good for doing everything that concerns the automobile.

THE FULL MOON IN CANCER

Danger: It is a gift, a blessing, and finally a pleasure to have many feelings. Often they are first perceived as a burden, and this can occur especially during a full moon in Cancer. The title of the well-known book by Robin Norwood, *Women Who Love Too Much*, epitomizes the power of this full moon. In reality, however, it is impossible to have too much love. At most, you don't have the right addresses or goals to turn to with your love, and in which you can invest it. And it is also easy to confuse love with self-sacrifice, as if in a partnership there should only be one opinion, or as if people were not contradictory in themselves.

Opportunity: The great challenge and potential happiness during a full moon in Cancer consists in being able to pass the test of spiritual conflicts and contradictory feelings and to get moving because of them. You will be in the wonderful position of being able to experience security and independence, safety and freedom together in love.

THE NEW MOON IN CANCER

Danger: From time to time the crustaceans in nature shed their protective armor, go into hiding, and finally acquire a new and transformed shell. During this time of transition and transformation, however, they are especially vulnerable, helpless, raw, and incomplete. This can be our situation during a new moon in Cancer. But don't despair!

Opportunity: The transformation (and the darkness) are only temporary.

Moon in Leo

Definition:	Leo—I will
Element:	Fire
Lunar phases:	Waxing moon from February until August, waning moon from August until February
Direction:	Descending lunar power
Energy:	Heat
Food:	Protein
Nature:	Fruits

HEALTH

The heart and the circulatory system, the eyes and the back, as well as the hair on the head and the face, are assigned to Leo. The principle of Leo is will. In Leo, you are able to pass the crucial test (or the ordeal by fire). In fact, you need such a test, so that your personal will (all the things you wish for) is purified by fire. When the cinders settle, the noble part is set free. The true will arises in and out of the flames. As a will to live, the will is the motor or the "heart" of the human being. Everything that promotes the joy of living also strengthens the will to live and the vital powers. This is crucial for the promotion of health when the moon is in Leo. Herbal teas for the heart and exercises for the back are certainly helpful, but the crucial factor is the joy of living. Physically, it affects the circulation, the eyes (and personal outlooks and insights), and the back (the other side that needs to be taken into account). It is not healthy, however, to say about everything, "Yes, I want to do it." It is much more sensible and beneficial to sort through and study your actual experiences—positive and negative. Then you will be able to find out what you need and want at the moment.

NATURE

The moon in Leo is the right time for sowing and cultivating fruit-bearing plants. With the exception of tomatoes, plants should not be watered at this time. In no case must artificial fertilizer be used. Recommended, on the other hand, are the gathering of herbs that strengthen the heart, the grafting of fruit trees (during a waxing moon), and the pruning of fruit-bearing plants.

FINANCES

The courage of Leo is indispensable in career and financial affairs. But an overestimation of your capabilities and a striving for dominance can be damaging. The "true will" is a complicated matter until you have found it. Then it becomes easier to handle. This is also true for business and finance. It is good to be bold, but not to take irresponsible risks. Rather, pay attention to what life has in store for you and where your "calling" lies. If you do this while the moon is in Leo, you will be enriched in every respect.

FAMILY

When the moon is in Leo, something has to move within the family—otherwise, things become boring. Excursions, games, and all forms of entertainment prove successful at this time, and bestow new energies on all members of the family. This is the right time to deal with cousins, with your own generation, and with its role.

LOVE

Wildness and dedication are the fuel of love. The moon in Leo is the right time to consider the needs of your heart and your drives. With drives or instincts it is the same as with feelings: you need to face your fears and desires and learn to distinguish between justified and unjustified fears as well as meaningful and meaningless desires. There is instinct in sexuality, of course, but it also exists as a kind of passion or obsessiveness in many other areas of life—including on the level of thinking: so-called "untamed thinking." In order not to get caught up in unhealthy ideas, you need to have much love towards yourself and your partner. Such love, however, will always come back to you, to your center, and to your "true will."

ADVENTURE

In earlier times, when they were used in a religious context, concepts such as a person's "calling" and "vocation" were very common. With the loss of religiosity, however, these concepts lost their validity for many people. And yet they exist—these pointers of fate that are much more than circumstantial events. And finally, the totality of life experiences teaches us that certain things work for us while others don't. From all of this, the "vocation" and "calling" in your own life begin to form. You could also talk of the goal or the task of life. Now, if your own will were to agree with this "true will" (in religious terms: the will of God), then you would have powers at your disposal that you would not have thought possible, and you would be able to score points that would eclipse everything else. With the moon in Leo, there is no greater adventure.

AT HOME

This is the right time to tidy up the children's room or the hobby tools and utensils. Beyond that, do only what is necessary and use the time for playing games. This is now more important than doing the dishes. Even doing the dishes, of course, can be transformed into sports, play, and excitement.

THE FULL MOON IN LEO

Danger: Restlessness and instinctiveness, apparently compulsive behavior that is difficult to direct. In fact, it is only during the full moon that this type of behavior is clearly visible. On other days and during other lunar phases, it is present as well, but more concealed.

Opportunity: It consists of achieving a better understanding of the will and the instinctual drives, and being able to distinguish what increases the pleasure of all participants in the long run, and what does not.

THE NEW MOON IN LEO

Danger: A critical, possibly unpleasant, time, if you are too fixated on the sun. You feel burnt out, as if your battery were run down. In reality, however, it's not a matter of switching off the circuit, but of switching over to something else.

Opportunity: From time to time, the will can and must be newly formulated in order for it to remain vital and strong.

Moon in Virgo

Definition:	Virgo—I analyze
Element:	Earth
Lunar phases:	Waxing moon from March until September, waning moon from September until March
Direction:	Descending lunar power
Energy:	Cold/rest
Food:	Salt
Nature:	Roots

HEALTH

The intestines and the pancreas are assigned to Virgo. In a metaphorical sense as well, the digestion, the selection, utilization, and excretion of food of any kind (even of mental, spiritual, and energetic or volitional "food") are called for at this time. Teas for the purification of the blood and for purging the intestines may contribute to your well-being. Apply everything that contributes to a healthy intestinal flora and drink sufficient fluids. In a metaphorical sense, digestion signifies sorting out one's problems. The key to this sign of the zodiac is "I analyze," but this does not refer only to theoretical analysis. The original meaning of the Greek word for analysis is also dissolution, solution, and reparation. This concerns the working out of contradictions, problems, and unresolved fears and desires. During the moon in Virgo, it is best to drop self-protective expressions such as "That's none of my business," "I'm not responsible for that," or "I don't know anything about that." Here we are dealing with people who, at the appropriate time, resolve their problems and fulfill their tasks without sweeping anything under the rug. It is not easy to do this amid the pressing issues of daily life, but it is possible. And it is the most important contribution to health and well-being that you can make when the moon is in this sign.

NATURE

The days when the moon is in Virgo (whether waxing or waning) are, of course, the best days for almost all jobs in the garden and in nature that have to do with cultivation. They are very well suited for all planting and transplanting, such as the planting of trees that are to grow very tall, of shrubs and hedges that are to grow quickly, of old trees that are to live in a new place, of balcony and indoor plants, of grass (during a waxing moon), and of cuttings. The days of Virgo are also a good time for fertilizing, distributing manure, for setting up a compost heap, and for setting fence posts. They are also good for controlling underground pests.

FINANCES

It is often said that the sign of Virgo is very frugal, that it is good with money but only with small amounts, and that it is quite pedantic and small-minded. In reality, however, there are numerous examples of financially and commercially very successful Virgo characters. The small-mindedness of this sign is probably more a rumor than a fact. What is undisputed is Virgo's ability to approach and conclude things in a very economical way. The greatest possible yield is achieved with the smallest possible means. It depends on the personality of the individual whether this wonderful ability expresses itself on a small or large financial scale. This is something to pay special attention to during a moon in Virgo.

FAMILY

The task and the strength of the moon in Virgo is to find solutions. Sometimes this may mean separating from your family in order to find a new family of your own. But it is important not to get stuck at this step. In a second step you need to settle your own needs and tasks, so that you gain enough maturity to be able to live successfully together with the other members of the family on a new and "liberated" basis. The moon in Virgo is the right time to deal with aunts and uncles, with other relatives, and with their money.

LOVE

In the area of love and partnership, is a pronounced sense of self beneficial or obnoxious? The need to deal with yourself, and make your own independence an indispensable condition of everything else, can sow seeds of discord in relationships and partnerships. Relationships that build on a mature sense of independence generally are and remain happy and long-lasting. The moon in Virgo offers the ideal opportunity and the right time for strengthening and acknowledging the independence, the autonomy, and the responsibility of each of the partners.

ADVENTURE

"We are longing to live individually and free like a tree and brotherly like a forest."

—Nazim Hikmet

The combination of a sense of community and a sense of self is and remains the greatest adventure for Virgo. The more areas of life that are shaped and fulfilled in accordance with this principle, the higher the pinnacle of happiness.

AT HOME

The moon in Virgo represents a good time for all activities in the household. Now is the right time for cutting hair. It is fun to tidy up, to beautify the home, and to care for the body. Giving and receiving massages (self-massage, if necessary: hand, head, foot, etc.) is a must while the moon is in Virgo!

THE FULL MOON IN VIRGO

Danger: It is said that "the master reveals himself in limiting himself." The more the Virgo qualities are based on excluding or disregarding others, the more irritating or even disrupting or disturbing can be the effect of the full moon in this sign. Whatever lies beyond your own reach makes itself felt very clearly in this lunar phase.

Opportunity: When you are concerned about difficult questions and problems, this lunar phase is ideal for finding good solutions.

THE NEW MOON IN VIRGO

Danger: A danger that should be mentioned here is a special lack of wit. You could experience a dullness or lack of ideas where you hardly know what to do with yourself and/or others. In this regard, everything depends on your personal consciousness. You need to remain especially alert and mentally fit, like those "wise maidens" who have their light ready even in the darkest night (as in the biblical parable of the wise and the foolish maidens).

Opportunity: With the right amount of watchfulness, the new moon in Virgo is an optimal time for distancing oneself from theoretical ideas and immersing oneself in actual events.

Moon in Libra

Definition:	Libra—I balance
Element:	Air
Lunar phases:	Waxing moon from April until October, waning moon from October until April
Direction:	Descending lunar power
Energy:	Air/light
Food:	Fat
Nature:	Flowers

HEALTH

The kidneys, bladder, and pelvic area are assigned to Libra. Sometimes the hips are also mentioned in connection with this sign, but, according to the traditional view, they belong more to Sagittarius. Libra's symbol of the scale also refers to the sense of equilibrium, whose most important organs are the ears, which in turn are assigned to Taurus. With problems of balance, therefore, we need to explore connections between Taurus and Libra. Inner balance depends on straightforwardness and uprightness. This is true in a moral as well as a physical sense. Physically, straightforwardness and uprightness have their effect in the spine. On the other hand, the need for harmony and conciliation is especially pronounced in this sign. A conflict may arise between the need for harmony and conciliation on the one hand, and straightforwardness and purposefulness on the other. If the balance between these and other efforts is disturbed, the equilibrium will be destroyed and dizziness might result. This is true in a physical sense (feelings of dizziness) as well as a metaphorical one. The crucial task here is to settle conflicts productively. Even in the physical sense, the task of sorting out or filtering good and bad is a task of the kidneys, which play a decisive role in the detoxification of the body. Hence, when the moon is in Libra, it is sensible to protect the areas of the kidneys and the bladder and to keep them warm. And it is just as important for health and well-being at this time to deal with conflicts in a kind and nonjudgmental manner. What is supposed to count as good and bad in a personal sense is not simply fixed, but changes, and must be defined anew. This requires empathy and tact, as well as consistency and endurance in regard to oneself as well as others. Criticism and self-criticism too must be brought into balance. Honesty and love of truth are not only moral problems: the sign of Libra teaches us that they are very practical virtues that have an immediate effect on our well-being.

NATURE

Sometimes it is said that the signs of Libra and Aquarius have little connection with nature and the world of plants, but this is not quite right. On days when the moon is in Libra or Aquarius, it is important consciously to grant nature some rest. Avoid the watering of indoor plants, for example. But all flowers and flowering plants indoors and outdoors may now be planted and cultivated. This is a good time to remove wilted leaves, dead shoots, and weeds.

FINANCES

The moon in Libra is generally the most suitable time for formulating goals, working out conflicts, and thereby arriving at decisions. This is a time to decide about all financial, career, and business-related matters. In every decision it is advisable to ask: "Whom does it benefit?" Here it is important to emphasize control and self-control.

FAMILY

This is the right time to practice more honesty, openness, and justice in the family, giving special attention to the personal needs of each member. The moon sign is now favorable for achieving a true understanding of these needs and for respecting them in communal decisions and activities.

LOVE

"Love thy neighbor as thyself"—nothing at first seems more difficult in the sign of Libra, and yet Libra offers the best preconditions for this goal. The crucial point is to understand your partner's personal needs—even needs that push your buttons and your intuition to its limit—because those needs can be very different from yours.

ADVENTURE

The greatest challenge and the greatest adventure with the moon in Libra is to find suitable goals. Suitable goals are those that unite a maximum number of interests and needs (your own and those of others), are great enough to achieve something significant, and attainable enough to be achieved within a certain time.

AT HOME

Airing the house and letting in a fresh breeze is needed now and has an especially wholesome effect. This is the right time to tidy up the desk, to take care of unpaid bills, and to put new ideas on paper.

THE FULL MOON IN LIBRA

Danger: The full moon makes many things visible (perhaps everything?) that normally act subliminally. If you look at them, you will gain insights into ideas and connections that are very far-reaching. Although they are always present, these connections are clear only now. If you do not deal carefully with this full moon, a presumptuous complacency may result. Instead of appreciating the miracle of creation and the adventures of life, you might simply be proud of yourself, which in the sign of the full moon will provide little enlightenment.

Opportunity: The opportunity lies beyond self-adulation but also beyond selfless modesty. An expansion of consciousness is now called for. Personal experience and insights lead towards new truths, which should be accepted and applied with kindness and consistency.

THE NEW MOON IN LIBRA

Danger: Misunderstandings, injustices, and disputes lurk as dangers. In order to avoid these, it is advisable either to withdraw or to start dealing with certain taboo areas of your own life.

Opportunity: Even unfamiliar topics, and those that have been taboo, can now be deciphered and understood, so that it becomes clear which taboos are meaningful and urgently needed and which are superfluous and harmful.

Moon in Scorpio

Definition:	Scorpio—I desire
Element:	Water
Lunar phases:	Waxing moon from May until November, waning moon from November until May
Direction:	Descending lunar power
Energy:	Water
Food:	Carbohydrates
Nature:	Leaves

HEALTH

The sexual organs and the excretory organs are assigned to this sign. The ovaries and the uterus, however, remain in the domain of Libra, and the intestinal area belongs to the sign of Virgo. The bladder and the urinary tract are also grouped in Libra. The position of the lower part of the abdomen is addressed just as much as relaxation or tension in the area of the genitalia or the buttocks. Here we are coming into taboo areas, and the right handling of these taboo subjects is decisive for health and well-being. In the area of the lower abdomen, we clearly feel physical exertion and relaxation, pleasure and displeasure, but we don't always attend to these feelings. Receiving and letting go, holding fast and pushing away, closing and opening, these movements occur physically in this area and represent a mental or spiritual state. When the moon is in Scorpio it is obvious that we are concerned with openness and tension not only in the area of sexuality, but also with excretion as well. It is important to pay attention to hitherto unconscious and unfamiliar sensations of body and soul, and it is a physical necessity to be concerned with our passions and desires! By occupying ourselves fully with the extremes of life and love, we will arrive at a healthy, personally mature position between the extremes. An exaggerated sense of shame can degenerate into prudishness, but an exaggerated shamelessness can end in insolence. You must determine for yourself where the happy mean lies. The more a healthy your attitude towards sexuality and the body, the more you will do for your overall health.

A healthy lower abdomen heals many other parts as well. For example, it literally removes the basis of migraine and hay fever. Tense toes and cold feet vanish if the lower abdomen is relaxed.

NATURE

Herbs—especially medicinal herbs—are very grateful for every kind of attention in this sign. Traditionally, the waxing moon in Scorpio is also said to be the right time for controlling garden slugs. Leafy vegetables may now be planted and cultivated. This is also the right time for mowing the lawn and watering indoor plants, as well as fertilizing flowers in the house and garden.

FINANCES

Unconscious needs and desires play a crucial role when the moon is in Scorpio. If you don't consider them, there is the danger of falling prey to illusions. But, if you have the ability to address and awaken subliminal desires, you will achieve significantly more than if only your intellect were involved. All of this also applies to success in financial matters, and in business and career.

FAMILY

As with finances, with family life too, everything depends on whether illusions are fostered or whether profound desires are considered and fulfilled. With the moon in Scorpio, areas lying in the shadows become illuminated and visible. This is the right time to achieve greater truthfulness and a more profound search for truth. And this is not basically a moral question. With the moon in Scorpio, we depend on truth and truthfulness in the sense of genuineness and authenticity, because only in this way are we able to understand our own passions and deeper fears.

LOVE

The moon in Scorpio brings profound feelings to the surface. Don't be surprised about a sudden vehemence that can express itself in hot lovemaking, devotion, the staking of claims, inseparability, disputes, affairs, or strict asceticism. Pay attention to the underlying needs in each case. Now is the right time to come to terms with deeper and more extreme feelings.

ADVENTURE

The greatest adventure with moon in Scorpio is satisfying your desires. Paradoxically, in Scorpio you can reach the pinnacle of happiness precisely when you can be happy without desires!

AT HOME

A good time for cleaning and doing the laundry. This is also true in a metaphorical sense. Now is the right time for settling unpaid bills, so that you can close the book on the past.

THE FULL MOON IN SCORPIO

Danger: Intense feelings, spiritual needs, and desires. The danger exists that you either identify with these and take yourself for a superman or superwoman (mistakenly), or that you despair of being able to handle these enormous feelings.

Opportunity: To be able to forgive and to pardon, to take your leave or to find reconciliation. Now is the right time to accept and understand even completely unfamiliar feelings.

THE NEW MOON IN SCORPIO

Danger: As with the new moon in Cancer, it is possible to fall into spiritual despair. Depression may have a stronger effect now than at other times, so it is advisable to seek help or simply wait two to three days until the moon is in another sign. Basically, this period concerns unfamiliar areas of the soul.

Opportunity: Feelings that normally are insufficiently acknowledged may now be given special consideration and expression. These may be feelings of mourning, anger, remorse, revenge, or other such things, but also unfamiliar longings, unexpected feelings of love, and a newly found courage for dealing with daily tasks and duties.

Moon in Sagittarius

Definition:	Sagittarius—I perceive
Element:	Fire
Lunar phases:	Waxing moon from June until December, waning moon from December until June
Direction:	Transition from descending to ascending lunar power
Energy:	Heat
Food:	Protein
Nature:	Fruits

HEALTH

The lumbar region and lumbar vertebrae are assigned to the sign of Sagittarius. Blood circulation in the lower back, in the hips, and further down in the legs and feet are likewise in the sign of Sagittarius. Generally, the entire region of the thighs is assigned to Sagittarius. Traditionally, the liver as an important organ of blood formation also belongs to Sagittarius. Troubles with the sciatic nerve, and usually lumbago as well, are connected with this sign.

Sagittarius does not only relate to the hunter and other marksmen who use weapons, but it also protects people and backs them up, acting like a sort of guardian angel. This sign in many respects is concerned with taking responsibility for yourself and others, protecting yourself and others, and watching over yourself and others—with a view to health and well-being. While in the previous sign of Scorpio we were dealing with deep-seated feelings and spiritual needs, in Sagittarius we are concerned with the formation and generation of drives and motivations, of grand designs, and of long-range goals. In Sagittarius, health and well-being depend on being able to live as a whole human being aligned with your inner fire and will. Disease or illness might occur if the opposition between desire and reality, between drive and deed, is too great. Then there is a crack, as with the case of lumbago, where the upper and lower body no longer fit properly. To watch over yourself, to take responsibility for yourself and others, means above all to promote development and growth in all.

NATURE
It is the right time for planting and cultivating all fruits and high-growing vegetables. Fruit trees and shrubs may now be pruned (during a waning moon in spring). It is good to fertilize when the moon is on the wane in Sagittarius. During these days, it's easier to control pests that live above the ground.

FINANCES
The moon in Sagittarius is good for success in every respect, because here it is especially easy to take up and deploy lots of energy. In order to realize the sought-after success and seize even unexpected opportunities for gain, you need to keep your eye on many simultaneous and complex movements, like an attentive gamekeeper or a passionate hunter. In the sign of Sagittarius, intuition and education are not a luxury, but an absolute necessity, for you to be able to assess the passing scene. This also applies to success in career and finances.

FAMILY
Something has to move here so that the heart and circulation remain in motion. Now is the right time to move mountains, provided the impetus comes from inner conviction and enthusiasm.

LOVE
The moon in Sagittarius is the right time for spontaneity, for the revelation and fulfillment of desires great and small. Now it is a time to consent to new experiences. You have the strength to test and expand limits. Let your creativity work and follow your passion—the sky's the limit!

ADVENTURE
Show your true colors and carry your own torch into the world—that is the pinnacle in Sagittarius: to take your own passions seriously and to live your own dreams even in the face of obstacles. What is at stake is a form of expression that can refer not only to sexuality, but also to every other area of life. It's a matter of making your own desires your guide and formulating a personal life plan that you put into action. The word "adventure"—which has the same root as the word "advent," and means "arrival," will then

become what it was always meant to be: an arrival at yourself, and an arrival at "God."

AT HOME

The more your own desires and guidelines actually determine your daily life, the less you need to run away when the moon is in Sagittarius. Only when there are enough adventures at home will the Sagittarian remain there.

THE FULL MOON IN SAGITTARIUS

Danger: During a full moon in Sagittarius, wishes and reality sometimes get mixed up. This is the danger. You are dreaming, and you don't even realize it. It is now very possible to dream, to interpret the dreams, and to make them a reality, but it is also more necessary than at any other time.

Opportunity: Far-reaching visions, life plans, and wishful thinking can become very pronounced at this time. This is fortunate and represents a great opportunity, for only the person who has great dreams will go long distances and hold out to the end even when difficulties appear.

THE NEW MOON IN SAGITTARIUS

Danger: The statement of Sagittarius is: "I perceive," and the new moon in Sagittarius is closer to the blind spot. Everyone has a blind spot (and usually several). The contents differ from one individual to another, but it is almost always the case that this blind spot covers feelings that are strong and very stubborn. It requires some experience and a conscious effort to be able to recognize the blind spot at all, and then correct it. The great danger in this phase is to be very affected, yet stubborn or clueless.

Opportunity: Being able to make great progress in dealing with the blind spot every time.

Moon in Capricorn

Definition:	Capricorn—I use
Element:	Earth
Lunar phases:	Waxing moon from July until January, waning moon from January until July
Direction:	Ascending lunar power
Energy:	Cold/rest
Food:	Salt
Nature:	Roots

HEALTH

The bones in the whole body—and especially the knees—are assigned to Capricorn, as are the coccyx and the bottom of the pelvis. The skin and the fingernails and toenails also belong to the Capricorn principle. The teeth are also influenced by Capricorn, but are really the domain of Taurus. The knees stand for personal flexibility and, on the other hand, for inflexibility. "All for one and one for all": Capricorn loves to put itself on a pedestal—and, paradoxically, it also loves to subordinate itself and "risk its hide." For Capricorn, this obviously does not constitute a contradiction. In Capricorn, this and other paradoxes are seldom a trifling matter. Rather, they relate to long—often lifelong—time spans. At times, Capricorn brings along a special sensitivity. Certain feelings of pleasure or displeasure, positive and negative stimulations, are sensed physically, often without being able to express themselves in any concrete way. There is an itch, a pinch, certain regions of the skin feel brittle, and so on. Don't ignore these sensations; they are important hints, revealing conditions that may possibly have long-term effects. Now you are offered the opportunity to perceive them consciously and to react to them appropriately. Moreover, it is true in Capricorn that whatever you do must have a tangible meaning. It must be useful. Among other things, this concerns the question of the meaning of life. This is not a philosophical luxury, but a necessity for long-term well-being and personal growth.

NATURE

The waning moon in Capricorn is the right time to pull weeds, create paths in the garden and the fields, plant, cultivate or preserve and store root and winter vegetables, and prune hedges, as well as controll subterranean pests.

FINANCES

An enormous ambition and, on the other hand, a complete surrender to destiny—an exaggerated activism and an exaggerated fatalism—both extremes are familiar to Capricorn. On the one hand, you want to distinguish yourself, while, on the other hand, you don't want to do it through what you are for yourself, but by what you can do for others and how you can optimize what already exists. The moon in Capricorn will support you in this .

FAMILY

Use these times when the moon is in Capricorn for fellowship. Mutual help and support are especially possible at this time, and bodily contact is now a must.

LOVE

Love when the moon is in Capricorn frequently touches on areas that are taboo. At this time, very longstanding topics may be addressed—things that perhaps should have been talked about long ago, or topics that you falsely assumed were settled. These and other issues can now be articulated. The opportunity now lies in really putting things in order and making peace. Now is also a good time to set love on an even more solid foundation. This is especially true for daily rules and habits, which should be abolished in favor of new principles that can gradually be adapted to personal needs and passions.

ADVENTURE

"Guard against feelings of arrogance and inferiority. Don't set the fox to keep the geese. Rather, cultivate the objects of your desire! Again and again, the love towards what is alive in you and your fellow human beings and the affection for the whole gamut of existing realities will show you what is essential at the moment. If you abide by this maxim, you will be at the

forefront of your time and at the height of your potentialities. Do you know a more enduring pinnacle of happiness?"

—Evelin Bürger and Johannes Fiebig

AT HOME

Now you need to care for your skin, your hair, and especially your nails! Check your long-term plans and continue writing them down. Make yourself useful. Use the time and take some time for yourself.

THE FULL MOON IN CAPRICORN

Danger: It is as if a light appeared in a dark night. Even very profound and inaccessible essential characteristics can become visible, and even unusually high mountaintops seem with in reach. The danger is that you will lose your sense of proportion.

Opportunity: Here the opportunity consists in finding your own morality, your own principles of life. In this sign, you are brought into the fortunate position of being able to recognize as many talents as possible, and to confirm as many taboos as are necessary. You see the wealth of human possibilities and the necessity of their meaningful limitations—more clearly than in any other sign.

THE NEW MOON IN CAPRICORN

Danger: This is "darkness in obscurity." Prophets of doom and pessimists are having a field day. Where before people saw the world through rose-colored glasses, with a superficially positive philosophy (a mere wishful thinking), now a useful realism can once again take charge.

Opportunity: We are still groping in the dark, but soon we will be able to discern new realities—hitherto unknown positive possibilities.

Moon in Aquarius

Definition:	Aquarius—I know
Element:	Air
Lunar phases:	Waxing moon from August until February, waning moon from February until August
Direction:	Ascending lunar power
Energy:	Air/light
Food:	Fat
Nature:	Flowers

HEALTH

The lower legs and the ankle joints are assigned to this sign of the zodiac, as are blood circulation in the legs, especially the lower legs, and possible ailments such as varicose veins. The significance of Aquarius is frequently misunderstood. The issue here is not water, for with Aquarius we are dealing with a sign of air. What nevertheless justifies and explains the name Aquarius is the metaphorical sense of "flow" and "stream." Aquarius deals with how we are able to move within the flow of time, the flow of thoughts, events, and so on. Aquarius has something to do with the kind of spirit, the kind of breath, and the kind of rhythm that flows through us. The inner flow in a human being is also expressed very clearly in the vegetative nervous system, in body posture, and in the electrical resistance of the skin. Here, as in the sign of Capricorn, it is long-term processes that determine health and well-being. Before clearly noticeable circulatory problems arise in the lower legs, for example, a few years have already passed. Smoking can be taken into consideration as a possible cause, but it is necessary to examine every attitude towards life and every habit that may lead to tension, to a constriction of the blood vessels, and/or a concentration of energy in the head rather than in the feet, in the nerves rather than in physical vitality. Aquarius states: "I know." The most important measure for preventing illness when the moon is in Aquarius should consist of being concerned about the things you do not know. The old saying "What the eye doesn't see, the heart doesn't grieve over" may be valid, but it can also make us complacent and inflexible.

NATURE

As with the moon in Libra, some advisors don't find much to say about the Aquarian moon regarding the house and garden, but, in fact, planting and cultivation of all flowering plants is very effective. And the moon in Aquarius is the best time for planning a garden and for landscaping outdoors as well as for creating artistic arrangements indoors. Still, at this time it's best to avoid watering indoor plants!

FINANCES

Balancing the books, reading balance sheets, understanding the inner structure of a company, becoming acquainted with work processes—these are all things that come easily at this time. Be sure to make use of the great impulses for planning and structuring offered by this sign for your financial affairs as well!

FAMILY

The moon in Aquarius is the right time for creative and friendly fellowship. The precondition for this is that the freedom and the proper rhythm of each family member is guaranteed. An essential element is also the preservation of a personal space into which each family member can withdraw.

LOVE

Now you need to do something so that your love is solidly grounded. Avoid superficiality and lack of commitment. The moon in Aquarius is the right time for a conscious handling of feelings and passions.

ADVENTURE

A great adventure in Aquarius is to come to understand your inner rhythms and the rhythms of life. With the moon in Aquarius, it is important not to be content with theoretical insights, but to experience the whole truth. Now you are able to handle great powers. Plan where you want to steer them.

AT HOME

If you have to organize a move or a complete home renovation, for example, and you have several obligations to fulfill simultaneously, this is the right time to do it with dash and within the deadline. Be sure to have good ventilation and clean air. This time also calls for diversions—crime stories, riddles, puzzles, and other thrilling pastimes.

THE FULL MOON IN AQUARIUS

Danger: Here, secrets are revealed, and great insights can be achieved. Even complicated matters reveal their inner order and clarity. This can be absolutely inspiring and uplifting. The danger lurks in a so-called inflation of the ego, a pride in your own vision without humility and respect for others.

Opportunity: The clarification and enlightenment of many complex matters and issues. Draw practical consequences from this knowledge, for the purpose of achieving more humanity, productivity, and love in daily life.

THE NEW MOON IN AQUARIUS

Danger: Here it becomes especially obvious what you do not know and what you cannot know. This can be the source not only of feelings of inferiority, but also of cynical and contemptuous reactions.

Opportunity: This consists in being able to grasp where the limits of knowledge and awareness lie. If you know what you know, you can at least sense what you do not know, and the personal quality of your life will become many times richer.

Moon in Pisces

Definition:	Pisces—I believe
Element:	Water
Lunar phases:	Waxing moon from September until March, waning moon from March until September
Direction:	Ascending lunar power
Energy:	Water
Food:	Carbohydrates
Nature:	Leaves

HEALTH

The feet are assigned to Pisces. All the other parts and organs of the body are mirrored in the feet. In addition, the feet also refer to your own stance—in the sense of your attachment to the ground, your view of the world, and your position in matters of religious faith. When we say, "How are you doing?" we are referring to a general sense of well-being, a sense that is connected with the feet. It is also involved with care and preventative measures in the area of health. The great moods of life have a lasting effect on the feet and on your entire sense of well-being. Joy, sorrow, loss, and fulfillment—these and other feelings want to be and must be lived in order to prevent a congestion of feelings, an accumulation and overflowing in the economy of the soul. The crux of personal well-being in this sign lies in the conscious handling of feelings and moods. Cultivated passions are not just a matter of romantic dreams. Here it becomes clear that profound feelings form the basis of a healthy and happy life. Everything that contributes to an even flow of feelings—not too little and not too much—is especially important when the moon is in Pisces.

NATURE

This is a favorable time for mowing the lawn, for planting leafy vegetables as well as for watering indoor plants, and for fertilizing all flowering plants. Some insist that the waning moon in Pisces especially is the right time for sowing potatoes. Whatever you sow will grow well now, and for a long time. Whatever you harvest now, however, should be consumed immediately.

FINANCES

The fact that Pisceans are emotional romantics does not mean at all that they are not good at dealing with money. As mentioned previously, meditation and market research are no longer mutually exclusive. The person with a lot of feeling is especially able to empathize with others. The attitudes and moods of target groups are more easy to determine when the moon is in this sign, which is why, for example, advertising campaigns work especially well in Pisces. Since monetary and financial matters always concern people as well, and since they always serve specific personal interests, Pisces is especially helpful with large groups and organizations.

FAMILY

Generally, the sign of Pisces is said to be very family-friendly. But it's easy to forget that, besides goldfish, there are also sharks. A great danger in the sign of Pisces is that individuals will subordinate themselves to the community or not regard themselves as individuals at all. This gives rise to compulsive fears—for example, the fear of stepping out of line—and also anger against those who nevertheless dare to do it. Profound feelings are thus a fertile ground for a pleasant and enjoyable family life, if the individual is guaranteed enough space for personal development, and when this self-actualization is pursued and promoted.

LOVE

Cultivated passions and strong feelings rule in Pisces. We are able to experience great happiness, and we are also able to give great happiness, when the moon is in Pisces. A lukewarm approach is not beneficial. To be cultivated means primarily to understand your feelings and passions. This is accomplished when you do not disavow fears and desires, but distinguish between them. Which desires make me stronger? Which desires make me weaker? Which fears do I want to face? And which would I rather avoid?

ADVENTURE

The greatest adventure in the sign of Pisces is to be able to sense, to experience, to question, and to re-experience your own calling and vocation. It is not possible to first interpret life dreams and then make them a reality, for these dreams after all concern your entire life span. Interpretation and realization are one. So, it is particularly important to examine what you believe. When you have examined and found your own standpoint, when you know what you believe in and why, then the moon in Pisces is the right time to commit and entrust yourself wholly to what you believe in and cherish.

AT HOME

Now is the right time for bathing, for swimming, for washing, and for drinking. With the moon in Pisces, it is not advisable to cut hair. The study of dreams is especially rewarding at this time, be they dreams at night or dreams of days remembered.

THE FULL MOON IN PISCES

Danger: The waves of the soul surge very high at this time. Depending on how much you like swimming, you will feel either very comfortable, like a fish in water, or you will be irritated because you have to regain your composure and get a firm hold.

Opportunity: It consists in an examination and questioning of your own life decisions and principles of faith. Dry and meaningless habits can now be washed away. Daily life will now be reoriented and focused on what is truly important to you.

THE NEW MOON IN PISCES

Danger: A period of low tide. This can be unpleasant, if previously you have only drawn on abundant resources. But you are closer to the pulse of life.

Opportunity: The individual course that you chart through the ocean can be developed particularly well during this phase. The full moon in Pisces connects you with the most important things in life—the basic questions of human existence. The new moon in Pisces, on the other hand, connects you with the most important personal things and the foundation of your own life.

TABLES AND CALENDAR

LUNAR TABLES 1920–1996

With the help of the following tables you'll be able to determine the moon sign for every important event in your past. You'll also be able to calculate the position of the moon at the time of your birth. This is your personal lunar sign.

This is how to find the moon's position for any date:

- From Table A, determine the lunar number A.
- In Table B on page 129, determine the lunar number B.
- Add the lunar numbers A and B.
- If the sum of lunar number A and lunar number B is greater than 360, subtract 1 × 360.
- Now you have calculated the desired lunar number.
- If you know the exact time of the event, add the correction from Table C on page 130.
- Using Table D on page 130, you will be able to determine your lunar interpretation number. It reveals which sign of the zodiac the moon was in at the time the event occurred.

Example: Larry R. got married at 10 a.m. on January 10, 1979.

Lunar number A	=	317
Lunar number B	=	121
Sum of A + B	=	438
Time from Table C	=	–3
Total	=	435
Subtract 1 × 360	=	–360
Lunar interpretation number	=	75

At the time of the wedding, the moon was in Gemini.

TABLE A/LUNAR NUMBER A

Month and year of the event

Year	January	February	March	April	May	June	July	August	September	October	November	December
1920	38	91	115	167	202	248	281	326	14	50	104	153
1921	194	241	249	294	325	10	44	94	148	286	237	271
1922	317	1	13	55	51	353	182	234	284	318	3	35
1923	80	128	138	188	227	280	316	3	46	78	123	159
1924	210	263	288	339	13	59	92	137	185	222	270	314
1925	4	51	59	103	129	179	214	265	319	357	48	81
1926	126	172	180	226	262	315	356	46	95	128	172	284
1927	250	299	306	359	38	90	126	172	216	248	294	330
1928	22	76	100	150	184	229	261	307	356	34	87	125
1929	175	221	229	273	304	350	25	76	130	168	218	252
1930	296	341	350	37	74	127	166	218	265	298	342	14
1931	59	139	117	170	208	261	295	341	25	58	105	142
1932	194	248	272	321	355	38	71	117	167	205	258	296
1933	345	31	38	82	114	160	196	248	332	240	29	63
1934	107	152	162	208	245	299	337	29	76	138	152	184
1935	230	280	288	341	20	72	106	251	196	229	277	314
1936	7	60	84	132	165	209	241	287	237	15	69	106
1937	155	200	208	252	285	331	8	60	114	151	200	233
1938	277	322	331	19	56	110	148	199	246	278	321	253
1939	40	90	99	153	191	242	276	322	6	39	88	126
1940	180	232	255	302	335	19	51	97	148	188	240	277
1941	352	10	18	61	95	142	180	232	286	223	10	43
1942	87	133	141	190	227	281	329	9	55	88	131	163
1943	211	262	272	325	3	53	87	132	176	210	260	298
1944	351	43	65	112	145	188	221	268	318	357	50	87
1945	135	180	188	232	266	314	352	45	97	134	381	214
1946	258	333	311	1	38	91	138	156	225	257	301	334
1947	22	73	84	136	175	224	258	302	347	22	72	126
1948	163	215	236	282	314	358	30	77	129	168	221	257

Year	January	February	March	April	May	June	July	August	September	October	November	December
1949	305	350	358	45	76	126	164	216	269	305	531	24
1950	65	114	121	171	289	263	300	350	35	67	111	144
1951	193	245	256	309	347	35	68	212	157	192	243	281
1952	335	25	46	92	124	167	200	248	300	339	31	68
1953	115	159	168	213	247	297	336	30	81	116	361	193
1954	237	283	291	241	29	73	111	160	205	237	281	315
1955	5	58	69	121	158	205	238	282	328	357	54	92
1956	145	196	214	262	293	337	11	60	112	151	203	239
1957	285	330	339	24	58	109	248	201	252	287	331	3
1958	47	93	101	142	196	244	281	330	15	47	92	126
1959	157	230	241	293	330	16	48	92	126	173	225	263
1960	316	6	26	71	103	147	181	231	284	323	14	50
1961	95	140	149	194	229	280	319	13	32	97	141	172
1962	216	264	272	323	2	55	92	140	184	217	263	298
1963	349	43	53	105	140	186	218	262	308	343	36	74
1964	126	176	196	241	273	317	353	43	96	135	186	221
1965	246	310	319	5	40	92	130	184	233	267	311	342
1966	27	74	83	135	174	227	263	310	355	28	74	110
1967	161	185	225	276	311	356	28	72	118	157	208	245
1968	297	346	6	51	83	129	164	215	268	307	357	31
1969	76	121	129	175	210	263	302	354	43	76	120	152
1970	197	245	255	307	347	38	74	121	165	198	245	281
1971	334	27	36	87	121	156	197	241	288	324	17	56
1972	107	156	176	221	254	300	335	27	81	119	168	202
1973	245	290	298	345	21	74	114	165	213	246	290	322
1974	7	57	66	120	158	210	245	291	325	8	55	92
1975	145	199	207	257	290	335	7	52	98	237	188	227
1976	278	326	347	32	63	110	147	200	253	291	339	12
1977	56	100	118	155	191	245	283	335	23	56	100	132
1978	178	227	238	292	331	22	56	101	145	179	226	263
1979	317	9	18	67	100	145	176	221	269	307	1	38
1980	23	136	157	201	234	282	319	11	65	102	150	182

Year	January	February	March	April	May	June	July	August	September	October	November	December
1981	226	270	278	325	2	55	94	245	193	226	270	303
1982	349	40	51	104	142	192	226	271	315	348	37	74
1983	127	181	188	237	270	314	346	31	80	118	171	210
1984	260	306	327	12	45	93	130	184	236	273	320	353
1985	36	80	88	136	173	226	266	316	353	36	80	113
1986	161	212	223	276	315	4	37	81	125	159	207	239
1987	296	351	359	46	80	124	156	203	253	291	344	23
1988	71	117	138	182	216	264	301	355	42	84	130	161
1989	205	250	258	306	344	38	77	127	173	206	250	284
1990	333	24	34	88	126	174	206	251	295	328	18	56
1991	109	162	168	217	250	294	327	14	64	103	156	194
1992	242	287	307	352	26	75	112	166	219	254	300	330
1993	15	60	66	119	156	210	249	297	344	16	61	95
1994	144	196	207	260	297	344	17	61	105	139	189	226
1995	278	331	340	27	59	105	132	185	236	275	328	6
1996	53	98	118	162	195	245	283	337	29	64	109	141

Note: If your lunar sign lies between two neighboring signs of the zodiac, the influences come from both signs.

TABLE B/LUNAR NUMBER B

Day of the event

Day	*Number*	*Day*	*Number*	*Day*	*Number*	*Day*	*Number*
1.	0	**8.**	94	**16.**	209	**24.**	309
2.	13	**9.**	107	**17.**	222	**25.**	322
3.	26	**10.**	121	**18.**	236	**26.**	336
4.	40	**11.**	134	**19.**	249	**27.**	349
5.	53	**12.**	148	**20.**	263	**28.**	3
6.	67	**13.**	161	**21.**	268	**29.**	16
7.	80	**14.**	175	**22.**	282	**30.**	30
		15.	288	**23.**	295	**31.**	43

TABLE C/CORRECTION

If the time of the event is between:

0–6 a.m.	6–12 a.m.	12–6 p.m.	6–12 p.m.
– 6	– 3	+ 3	+ 6

TABLE D/LUNAR INTERPRETATION NUMBER

Your lunar number lies between	It corresponds to the moon in
355–5	Pisces/Aries
6–24	Aries
25–34	Aries/Taurus
35–54	Taurus
55–64	Taurus/Gemini
65–84	Gemini
85–96	Gemini/Cancer
97–114	Cancer
115–124	Cancer/Leo
125–144	Leo
145–154	Leo/Virgo
155–174	Virgo
175–184	Virgo/Libra
185–204	Libra
205–214	Libra/Scorpio
215–234	Scorpio
235–244	Scorpio/Sagittarius
245–264	Sagittarius
265–274	Sagittarius/Capricorn
275–294	Capricorn
295–304	Capricorn/Aquarius
305–324	Aquarius
325–334	Aquarius/Pisces
335–354	Pisces

LUNAR CALENDAR 1997–2020

Aries	ram
Taurus	bull
Gemini	twins
Cancer	crab
Leo	lion
Virgo	virgin
Libra	scales
Scorpio	scorpion
Sagittarius	archer
Capricorn	goat
Aquarius	waterbearer
Pisces	fish

Days of the full moon have a frame around them.

Days of the new moon are indicated in black.

The entries refer to 0 hour Greenwich Mean Time (the first hour of the day). If the event you are looking for took place in New York, for example, the entries would refer to 7 p.m. the day before. If it took place in Chicago, they would refer to 6 p.m.; Denver, 5 p.m.; and Los Angeles, 4 p.m.

1997

	January	February	March	April	May	June	July	August	September	October	November	December
1.	W♍	S♏	S♏	T♑	T♒	S♈	T♉	F♋	M♍	W♎	S♏	M♐
2.	T♎	S♏	S♐	W♑	F♓	M♈	W♊	S♋	T♍	T♎	S♏	T♑
3.	F♎	M♐	M♐	T♒	S♓	T♉	T♊	S♌	W♍	F♎	M♐	W♑
4.	S♏	T♐	T♑	F♒	S♈	W♉	F♋	M♌	T♎	S♏	T♐	T♒
5.	S♏	W♑	W♑	S♓	M♈	T♊	S♋	T♍	F♎	S♏	W♑	F♒
6.	M♐	T♑	T♒	S♓	T♈	F♊	S♋	W♍	S♎	M♐	T♑	S♒
7.	T♐	F♒	F♒	M♈	W♉	S♋	M♌	T♍	S♏	T♐	F♒	S♓
8.	W♑	S♒	S♓	T♈	T♊	S♋	T♌	F♎	M♏	W♐	S♒	M♓
9.	T♑	S♓	S♓	W♉	F♊	M♌	W♍	S♎	T♐	T♑	S♓	T♈
10.	F♒	M♓	M♈	T♉	S♊	T♌	T♍	S♏	W♐	F♑	M♓	W♈
11.	S♒	T♈	T♈	F♊	S♋	W♌	F♍	M♏	T♐	S♒	T♓	T♉
12.	S♓	W♈	W♉	S♊	M♋	T♍	S♎	T♏	F♑	S♒	W♈	F♉
13.	M♓	T♉	T♉	S♋	T♌	F♍	S♎	W♐	S♑	M♓	T♈	S♊
14.	T♈	F♉	F♉	M♋	W♌	S♎	M♏	T♐	S♒	T♓	F♉	S♊
15.	W♈	S♊	S♊	T♋	T♍	S♎	T♏	F♑	M♒	W♈	S♉	M♋
16.	T♈	S♊	S♊	W♌	F♍	M♎	W♏	S♑	T♓	T♈	S♊	T♋
17.	F♉	M♊	M♋	T♌	S♍	T♏	T♐	S♒	W♓	F♉	M♊	W♌
18.	S♉	T♋	T♋	F♍	S♎	W♏	F♐	M♒	T♈	S♉	T♋	T♌
19.	S♊	W♋	W♌	S♍	M♎	T♐	S♑	T♓	F♈	S♊	W♋	F♌
20.	M♊	T♌	T♌	S♍	T♏	F♐	S♑	W♓	S♉	M♊	T♌	S♍
21.	T♋	F♌	F♌	M♎	W♏	S♑	M♒	T♈	S♉	T♋	F♌	S♍
22.	W♋	S♍	S♍	T♏	T♐	S♑	T♒	F♈	M♊	W♋	S♌	M♎
23.	T♌	S♍	S♍	W♏	F♐	M♒	W♓	S♉	T♊	T♋	S♍	T♎
24.	F♌	M♍	M♎	T♏	S♐	T♒	T♓	S♉	W♋	F♌	M♍	W♎
25.	S♌	T♎	T♎	F♐	S♑	W♒	F♈	M♊	T♋	S♌	T♎	T♏
26.	S♍	W♎	W♎	S♐	M♑	T♓	S♈	T♊	F♌	S♍	W♎	F♏
27.	M♍	T♎	T♏	S♑	T♒	F♓	S♉	W♊	S♌	M♍	T♎	S♐
28.	T♍	F♏	F♏	M♑	W♒	S♈	M♉	T♋	S♌	T♍	F♏	S♐
29.	W♎		S♐	T♑	T♓	S♈	T♊	F♋	M♍	W♎	S♏	M♑
30.	T♎		S♐	W♒	F♓	M♉	W♊	S♌	T♍	T♎	S♐	T♑
31.	F♏		M♐		S♈		T♊	S♌		F♏		W♑

1998

January	February	March	April	May	June	July	August	September	October	November	December	
T ♒	S ♈	S ♈	W ♊	F ♋	M ♌	W ♎	S ♏	T ♐	T ♒	S ♓	T ♉	1.
F ♒	M ♈	M ♈	T ♊	S ♋	T ♍	T ♎	S ♏	W ♑	F ♒	M ♈	W ♉	2.
S ♓	T ♉	T ♉	F ♋	S ♌	W ♍	F ♎	M ♐	T ♑	S ♓	T ♈	T ♊	3.
S ♓	W ♉	W ♉	S ♋	M ♌	T ♎	S ♏	T ♐	F ♒	S ♓	W ♉	F ♊	4.
M ♈	T ♉	T ♊	S ♋	T ♍	F ♎	S ♏	W ♑	S ♒	M ♈	T ♉	S ♋	5.
T ♈	F ♊	F ♊	M ♌	W ♍	S ♎	M ♐	T ♑	S ♓	T ♈	F ♊	S ♋	6.
W ♉	S ♊	S ♋	T ♌	T ♍	S ♏	T ♐	F ♒	M ♓	W ♉	S ♊	M ♌	7.
T ♉	S ♋	S ♋	W ♍	F ♎	M ♏	W ♐	S ♒	T ♈	T ♉	S ♋	T ♌	8.
F ♊	M ♋	M ♌	T ♍	S ♎	T ♐	T ♑	S ♒	W ♈	F ♊	M ♋	W ♌	9.
S ♊	T ♌	T ♌	F ♍	S ♏	W ♐	F ♑	M ♓	T ♉	S ♊	T ♌	T ♍	10.
S ♊	W ♌	W ♌	S ♎	M ♏	T ♐	S ♒	T ♓	F ♉	S ♊	W ♌	F ♍	11.
M ♋	T ♌	T ♍	S ♎	T ♏	F ♑	S ♒	W ♈	S ♊	M ♋	T ♍	S ♎	12.
T ♋	F ♍	F ♍	M ♏	W ♐	S ♑	M ♓	T ♈	S ♊	T ♋	F ♍	S ♎	13.
W ♌	S ♍	S ♎	T ♏	T ♐	S ♒	T ♓	F ♉	M ♋	W ♌	S ♍	M ♎	14.
T ♌	S ♎	S ♎	W ♏	F ♑	M ♒	W ♈	S ♉	T ♋	T ♌	S ♎	T ♏	15.
F ♍	M ♎	M ♎	T ♐	S ♑	T ♓	T ♈	S ♊	W ♋	F ♍	M ♎	W ♏	16.
S ♍	T ♎	T ♏	F ♐	S ♑	W ♓	F ♈	M ♊	T ♌	S ♍	T ♏	T ♐	17.
S ♍	W ♏	W ♏	S ♑	M ♒	T ♈	S ♉	T ♋	F ♌	S ♍	W ♏	F ♐	18.
M ♎	T ♏	T ♐	S ♑	T ♒	F ♈	S ♉	W ♋	S ♍	M ♎	T ♏	S ♐	19.
T ♎	F ♐	F ♐	M ♒	W ♓	S ♉	M ♊	T ♌	S ♍	T ♎	F ♐	S ♑	20.
W ♏	S ♐	S ♐	T ♒	T ♓	S ♉	T ♊	F ♌	M ♎	W ♏	S ♐	M ♑	21.
T ♏	S ♑	S ♑	W ♒	F ♈	M ♊	W ♋	S ♌	T ♎	T ♏	S ♑	T ♒	22.
F ♏	M ♑	M ♑	T ♓	S ♈	T ♊	T ♌	S ♍	W ♎	F ♏	M ♑	W ♒	23.
S ♐	T ♑	T ♒	F ♓	S ♉	W ♋	F ♌	M ♍	T ♏	S ♐	T ♑	T ♓	24.
S ♐	W ♒	W ♒	S ♈	M ♊	T ♋	S ♌	T ♎	F ♏	S ♐	W ♒	F ♓	25.
M ♑	T ♓	T ♓	S ♈	T ♊	F ♋	S ♍	W ♎	S ♐	M ♑	T ♒	S ♓	26.
T ♑	F ♓	F ♓	M ♉	W ♊	S ♌	M ♍	T ♎	S ♐	T ♑	F ♓	S ♈	27.
W ♒	S ♓	S ♈	T ♉	T ♋	S ♌	T ♍	F ♏	M ♐	W ♑	S ♓	M ♈	28.
T ♒		S ♈	W ♊	F ♋	M ♍	W ♎	S ♏	T ♑	T ♒	S ♈	T ♉	29.
F ♓		M ♉	T ♊	S ♌	T ♍	T ♎	S ♐	W ♑	F ♒	M ♈	W ♉	30.
S ♓		T ♉		S ♌		F ♏	M ♐		S ♓		T ♊	31.

1999

	January	February	March	April	May	June	July	August	September	October	November	December
1.	F ♊	M ♌	M ♌	T ♎	S ♏	T ♐	T ♒	S ♓	W ♉	F ♊	M ♌	W ♍
2.	S ♋	T ♌	T ♍	F ♎	S ♏	W ♑	F ♒	M ♈	T ♉	S ♋	T ♌	T ♎
3.	S ♋	W ♍	W ♍	S ♏	M ♐	T ♑	S ♒	T ♈	F ♊	S ♋	W ♍	F ♎
4.	M ♌	T ♍	T ♎	S ♏	T ♐	F ♒	S ♓	W ♉	S ♊	M ♌	T ♍	S ♎
5.	T ♌	F ♎	F ♎	M ♏	W ♑	S ♒	M ♓	T ♉	S ♋	T ♌	F ♎	S ♏
6.	W ♍	S ♎	S ♎	T ♐	T ♑	S ♓	T ♈	F ♊	M ♋	W ♍	S ♎	M ♏
7.	T ♍	S ♏	S ♏	W ♐	F ♑	M ♓	W ♈	S ♊	T ♌	T ♍	S ♏	T ♐
8.	F ♍	M ♏	M ♏	T ♑	S ♒	T ♓	T ♉	S ♊	W ♌	F ♍	M ♏	W ♐
9.	S ♎	T ♏	T ♐	F ♑	S ♒	W ♈	F ♉	M ♋	T ♍	S ♎	T ♏	T ♐
10.	S ♎	W ♐	W ♐	S ♑	M ♓	T ♈	S ♊	T ♋	F ♍	S ♎	W ♐	F ♑
11.	M ♏	T ♐	T ♐	S ♒	T ♓	F ♉	S ♊	W ♌	S ♎	M ♏	T ♐	S ♑
12.	T ♏	F ♑	F ♑	M ♒	W ♈	S ♉	M ♋	T ♌	S ♎	T ♏	F ♑	S ♒
13.	W ♏	S ♑	S ♑	T ♓	T ♈	S ♊	T ♋	F ♍	M ♎	W ♏	S ♑	M ♒
14.	T ♐	S ♑	S ♒	W ♓	F ♉	M ♊	W ♌	S ♍	T ♏	T ♐	S ♑	T ♒
15.	F ♐	M ♒	M ♒	T ♈	S ♉	T ♋	T ♌	S ♎	W ♏	F ♐	M ♒	W ♓
16.	S ♑	T ♒	T ♓	F ♈	S ♊	W ♋	F ♍	M ♎	T ♐	S ♑	T ♒	T ♓
17.	S ♑	W ♓	W ♓	S ♉	M ♊	T ♌	S ♍	T ♏	F ♐	S ♑	W ♓	F ♈
18.	M ♒	T ♓	T ♓	S ♉	T ♋	F ♌	S ♍	W ♏	S ♐	M ♑	T ♓	S ♈
19.	T ♒	F ♈	F ♈	M ♊	W ♋	S ♍	M ♎	T ♏	S ♑	T ♒	F ♓	S ♉
20.	W ♒	S ♈	S ♈	T ♊	T ♌	S ♍	T ♎	F ♐	M ♑	W ♒	S ♈	M ♉
21.	T ♓	S ♉	S ♉	W ♋	F ♌	M ♎	W ♏	S ♐	T ♒	T ♓	S ♈	T ♊
22.	F ♓	M ♉	M ♉	T ♋	S ♌	T ♎	T ♏	S ♑	W ♒	F ♓	M ♉	W ♋
23.	S ♈	T ♊	T ♊	F ♌	S ♍	W ♎	F ♏	M ♑	T ♒	S ♈	T ♊	T ♋
24.	S ♈	W ♊	W ♊	S ♌	M ♍	T ♏	S ♐	T ♑	F ♓	S ♈	W ♊	F ♋
25.	M ♉	T ♋	T ♋	S ♍	T ♎	F ♏	S ♐	W ♒	S ♓	M ♉	T ♊	S ♌
26.	T ♉	F ♋	F ♋	M ♍	W ♎	S ♐	M ♑	T ♒	S ♈	T ♉	F ♋	S ♌
27.	W ♊	S ♋	S ♌	T ♍	T ♎	S ♐	T ♑	F ♓	M ♈	W ♊	S ♋	M ♍
28.	T ♊	S ♌	S ♌	W ♎	F ♏	M ♑	W ♒	S ♓	T ♉	T ♊	S ♌	T ♍
29.	F ♋		M ♍	T ♎	S ♏	T ♑	T ♒	S ♈	W ♉	F ♋	M ♌	W ♍
30.	S ♋		T ♍	F ♏	S ♐	W ♑	F ♒	M ♈	T ♊	S ♋	T ♍	T ♎
31.	S ♌		W ♎		M ♐		S ♓	T ♈		S ♌		F ♎

2000

January	February	March	April	May	June	July	August	September	October	November	December	
S	T	W	S	M	T	S	T	F	S	W	F	1.
S	W	T	S	T	F	S	W	S	M	T	S	2.
M	T	F	M	W	S	M	T	S	T	F	S	3.
T	F	S	T	T	S	T	F	M	W	S	M	4.
W	S	S	W	F	M	W	S	T	T	S	T	5.
T	S	M	T	S	T	T	S	W	F	M	W	6.
F	M	T	F	S	W	F	M	T	S	T	T	7.
S	T	W	S	M	T	S	T	F	S	W	F	8.
S	W	T	S	T	F	S	W	S	M	T	S	9.
M	T	F	M	W	S	M	T	S	T	F	S	10.
T	F	S	T	T	S	T	F	M	W	S	M	11.
W	S	S	W	F	M	W	S	T	T	S	T	12.
T	S	M	T	S	T	T	S	W	F	M	W	13.
F	M	T	F	S	W	F	M	T	S	T	T	14.
S	T	W	S	M	T	S	T	F	S	W	F	15.
S	W	T	S	T	F	S	W	S	M	T	S	16.
M	T	F	M	W	S	M	T	S	T	F	S	17.
T	F	S	T	T	S	T	F	M	W	S	M	18.
W	S	S	W	F	M	W	S	T	T	S	T	19.
T	S	M	T	S	T	T	S	W	F	M	W	20.
F	M	T	F	S	W	F	M	T	S	T	T	21.
S	T	W	S	M	T	S	T	F	S	W	F	22.
S	W	T	S	T	F	S	W	S	M	T	S	23.
M	T	F	M	W	S	M	T	S	T	F	S	24.
T	F	S	T	T	S	T	F	M	W	S	M	25.
W	S	S	W	F	M	W	S	T	T	S	T	26.
T	S	M	T	S	T	T	S	W	F	M	W	27.
F	M	T	F	S	W	F	M	T	S	T	T	28.
S	T	W	S	M	T	S	T	F	S	W	F	29.
S		T	S	T	F	S	W	S	M	T	S	30.
M		F		W		M	T		T		S	31.

2001

	January	February	March	April	May	June	July	August	September	October	November	December
1.	M ♓	T ♉	T ♉	S ♋	T ♌	F ♎	S ♏	W ♑	S ♒	M ♓	T ♉	S ♊
2.	T ♈	F ♉	F ♉	M ♋	W ♌	S ♎	M ♏	T ♑	S ♒	T ♈	F ♉	S ♊
3.	W ♈	S ♊	S ♊	T ♌	T ♍	S ♏	T ♐	F ♑	M ♓	W ♈	S ♊	M ♋
4.	T ♈	S ♊	S ♊	W ♌	F ♍	M ♏	W ♐	S ♒	T ♓	T ♈	S ♊	T ♋
5.	F ♉	M ♋	M ♋	T ♍	S ♎	T ♐	T ♑	S ♒	W ♈	F ♉	M ♊	W ♌
6.	S ♉	T ♋	T ♋	F ♍	S ♎	W ♐	F ♑	M ♓	T ♈	S ♉	T ♋	T ♌
7.	S ♊	W ♌	W ♌	S ♎	M ♏	T ♐	S ♒	T ♓	F ♈	S ♊	W ♋	F ♍
8.	M ♊	T ♌	T ♌	S ♎	T ♏	F ♑	S ♒	W ♓	S ♉	M ♊	T ♌	S ♍
9.	T ♋	F ♍	F ♍	M ♏	W ♐	S ♑	M ♒	T ♈	S ♉	T ♋	F ♌	S ♎
10.	W ♋	S ♍	S ♍	T ♏	T ♐	S ♒	T ♓	F ♈	M ♊	W ♋	S ♍	M ♎
11.	T ♌	S ♎	S ♎	W ♏	F ♑	M ♒	W ♓	S ♉	T ♊	T ♋	S ♍	T ♏
12.	F ♌	M ♎	M ♎	T ♐	S ♑	T ♒	T ♓	S ♉	W ♋	F ♌	M ♎	W ♏
13.	S ♍	T ♎	T ♏	F ♐	S ♑	W ♓	F ♈	M ♉	T ♋	S ♌	T ♎	T ♏
14.	S ♍	W ♏	W ♏	S ♑	M ♒	T ♓	S ♈	T ♊	F ♌	S ♍	W ♏	F ♐
15.	M ♎	T ♏	T ♐	S ♑	T ♒	F ♈	S ♉	W ♊	S ♌	M ♍	T ♏	S ♐
16.	T ♎	F ♐	F ♐	M ♑	W ♓	S ♈	M ♉	T ♋	S ♍	T ♎	F ♐	S ♑
17.	W ♏	S ♐	S ♐	T ♒	T ♓	S ♈	T ♊	F ♋	M ♍	W ♎	S ♐	M ♑
18.	T ♏	S ♑	S ♑	W ♒	F ♓	M ♉	W ♊	S ♌	T ♎	T ♏	S ♐	T ♒
19.	F ♏	M ♑	M ♑	T ♓	S ♈	T ♉	T ♋	S ♌	W ♎	F ♏	M ♑	W ♒
20.	S ♐	T ♑	T ♒	F ♓	S ♈	W ♊	F ♋	M ♍	T ♏	S ♐	T ♑	T ♒
21.	S ♐	W ♒	W ♒	S ♓	M ♉	T ♊	S ♌	T ♍	F ♏	S ♐	W ♒	F ♓
22.	M ♑	T ♒	T ♒	S ♈	T ♉	F ♋	S ♌	W ♎	S ♐	M ♑	T ♒	S ♓
23.	T ♑	F ♓	F ♓	M ♈	W ♊	S ♋	M ♍	T ♎	S ♐	T ♑	F ♓	S ♈
24.	W ♑	S ♓	S ♓	T ♉	T ♊	S ♌	T ♍	F ♏	M ♐	W ♑	S ♓	M ♈
25.	T ♒	S ♓	S ♈	W ♉	F ♊	M ♌	W ♎	S ♏	T ♑	T ♒	S ♓	T ♈
26.	F ♒	M ♈	M ♈	T ♊	S ♋	T ♍	T ♎	S ♐	W ♑	F ♒	M ♈	W ♉
27.	S ♓	T ♈	T ♈	F ♊	S ♋	W ♍	F ♎	M ♐	T ♒	S ♓	T ♈	T ♉
28.	S ♓	W ♉	W ♉	S ♋	M ♌	T ♎	S ♏	T ♐	F ♒	S ♓	W ♉	F ♊
29.	M ♓		T ♉	S ♋	T ♌	F ♎	S ♏	W ♑	S ♒	M ♓	T ♉	S ♊
30.	T ♈		F ♊	M ♌	W ♍	S ♏	M ♐	T ♑	S ♓	T ♈	F ♉	S ♋
31.	W ♈		S ♊		T ♍		T ♐	F ♒		W ♈		M ♋

2002

January	February	March	April	May	June	July	August	September	October	November	December	
T ♌	F ♍	F ♎	M ♏	W ♑	S ♒	M ♓	T ♉	S ♊	T ♋	F ♍	S ♎	1.
W ♌	S ♎	S ♎	T ♐	T ♑	S ♓	T ♈	F ♉	M ♋	W ♌	S ♍	M ♏	2.
T ♍	S ♎	S ♏	W ♐	F ♑	M ♓	W ♈	S ♉	T ♋	T ♌	S ♎	T ♏	3.
F ♍	M ♏	M ♏	T ♑	S ♒	T ♓	T ♈	S ♊	W ♋	F ♍	M ♏	W ♐	4.
S ♍	T ♏	T ♐	F ♑	S ♒	W ♈	F ♉	M ♊	T ♌	S ♍	T ♏	T ♐	5.
S ♎	W ♐	W ♐	S ♒	M ♓	T ♈	S ♉	T ♋	F ♌	S ♎	W ♏	F ♑	6.
M ♎	T ♐	T ♐	S ♒	T ♓	F ♈	S ♊	W ♋	S ♍	M ♎	T ♐	S ♑	7.
T ♏	F ♑	F ♑	M ♒	W ♓	S ♉	M ♊	T ♌	S ♍	T ♏	F ♐	S ♒	8.
W ♏	S ♑	S ♑	T ♓	T ♈	S ♉	T ♊	F ♌	M ♎	W ♏	S ♑	M ♒	9.
T ♐	S ♑	S ♒	W ♓	F ♈	M ♊	W ♋	S ♍	T ♎	T ♐	S ♑	T ♒	10.
F ♐	M ♒	M ♒	T ♈	S ♉	T ♊	T ♋	S ♍	W ♏	F ♐	M ♒	W ♓	11.
S ♑	T ♒	T ♒	F ♈	S ♉	W ♋	F ♌	M ♎	T ♏	S ♑	T ♒	T ♓	12.
S ♑	W ♓	W ♓	S ♈	M ♉	T ♋	S ♌	T ♎	F ♐	S ♑	W ♓	F ♈	13.
M ♑	T ♓	T ♓	S ♉	T ♊	F ♌	S ♍	W ♏	S ♐	M ♑	T ♓	S ♈	14.
T ♒	F ♓	F ♈	M ♉	W ♊	S ♌	M ♍	T ♏	S ♑	T ♒	F ♓	S ♈	15.
W ♒	S ♈	S ♈	T ♊	T ♋	S ♌	T ♎	F ♐	M ♑	W ♒	S ♈	M ♉	16.
T ♓	S ♈	S ♈	W ♊	F ♋	M ♍	W ♎	S ♐	T ♒	T ♓	S ♈	T ♉	17.
F ♓	M ♉	M ♉	T ♊	S ♌	T ♍	T ♏	S ♐	W ♒	F ♓	M ♉	W ♊	18.
S ♓	T ♉	T ♉	F ♋	S ♌	W ♎	F ♏	M ♑	T ♒	S ♈	T ♉	T ♊	19.
S ♈	W ♉	W ♊	S ♋	M ♍	T ♎	S ♐	T ♑	F ♓	S ♈	W ♉	F ♋	20.
M ♈	T ♊	T ♊	S ♌	T ♍	F ♏	S ♐	W ♒	S ♓	M ♈	T ♊	S ♋	21.
T ♉	F ♊	F ♊	M ♌	W ♍	S ♏	M ♑	T ♒	S ♈	T ♉	F ♊	S ♋	22.
W ♉	S ♋	S ♋	T ♍	T ♎	S ♐	T ♑	F ♓	M ♈	W ♉	S ♋	M ♌	23.
T ♉	S ♋	S ♋	W ♍	F ♎	M ♑	W ♒	S ♓	T ♈	T ♉	S ♋	T ♌	24.
F ♊	M ♌	M ♌	T ♎	S ♏	T ♑	T ♒	S ♓	W ♉	F ♊	M ♋	W ♍	25.
S ♊	T ♌	T ♌	F ♎	S ♐	W ♑	F ♒	M ♈	T ♉	S ♊	T ♌	T ♍	26.
S ♋	W ♍	W ♍	S ♏	M ♐	T ♒	S ♓	T ♈	F ♊	S ♋	W ♌	F ♎	27.
M ♌	T ♍	T ♎	S ♏	T ♐	F ♒	S ♓	W ♉	S ♊	M ♋	T ♍	S ♎	28.
T ♌		F ♎	M ♐	W ♑	S ♒	M ♓	T ♉	S ♊	T ♌	F ♍	S ♏	29.
W ♌		S ♎	T ♐	T ♑	S ♓	T ♈	F ♉	M ♋	W ♌	S ♎	M ♏	30.
T ♍		S ♏		F ♒		W ♈	S ♊		T ♍		T ♐	31.

2003

	January	February	March	April	May	June	July	August	September	October	November	December
1.	W ♐	S ♒	S ♒	T ♈	T ♉	S ♊	T ♋	F ♍	M ♏	W ♐	S ♒	M ♓
2.	T ♑	S ♒	S ♒	W ♈	F ♉	M ♋	W ♌	S ♍	T ♏	T ♐	S ♒	T ♓
3.	F ♑	M ♓	M ♓	T ♈	S ♉	T ♋	T ♌	S ♎	W ♐	F ♑	M ♓	W ♈
4.	S ♑	T ♓	T ♓	F ♉	S ♊	W ♋	F ♍	M ♎	T ♐	S ♑	T ♓	T ♈
5.	S ♒	W ♓	W ♈	S ♉	M ♊	T ♌	S ♍	T ♏	F ♑	S ♒	W ♓	F ♉
6.	M ♒	T ♈	T ♈	S ♊	T ♋	F ♌	S ♍	W ♏	S ♑	M ♒	T ♈	S ♉
7.	T ♓	F ♈	F ♈	M ♊	W ♋	S ♌	M ♎	T ♐	S ♑	T ♓	F ♈	S ♉
8.	W ♓	S ♉	S ♉	T ♊	T ♋	S ♍	T ♎	F ♐	M ♒	W ♓	S ♉	M ♊
9.	T ♈	S ♉	S ♉	W ♋	F ♌	M ♍	W ♏	S ♑	T ♒	T ♈	S ♉	T ♊
10.	F ♈	M ♉	M ♊	T ♋	S ♌	T ♎	T ♏	S ♑	W ♓	F ♈	M ♉	W ♊
11.	S ♈	T ♊	T ♊	F ♌	S ♍	W ♎	F ♐	M ♒	T ♓	S ♈	T ♊	T ♋
12.	S ♉	W ♊	W ♊	S ♌	M ♍	T ♏	S ♐	T ♒	F ♈	S ♉	W ♊	F ♋
13.	M ♉	T ♋	T ♋	S ♌	T ♎	F ♏	S ♑	W ♒	S ♈	M ♉	T ♋	S ♌
14.	T ♊	F ♋	F ♋	M ♍	W ♎	S ♐	M ♑	T ♓	S ♈	T ♊	F ♋	S ♌
15.	W ♊	S ♋	S ♌	T ♍	T ♏	S ♑	T ♒	F ♓	M ♉	W ♊	S ♋	M ♍
16.	T ♊	S ♌	S ♌	W ♎	F ♏	M ♑	W ♒	S ♈	T ♉	T ♊	S ♌	T ♍
17.	F ♋	M ♌	M ♍	T ♎	S ♐	T ♑	T ♓	S ♈	W ♊	F ♋	M ♌	W ♍
18.	S ♋	T ♍	T ♍	F ♏	S ♐	W ♒	F ♓	M ♉	T ♊	S ♋	T ♍	T ♎
19.	S ♌	W ♍	W ♎	S ♏	M ♑	T ♒	S ♈	T ♉	F ♊	S ♌	W ♍	F ♎
20.	M ♌	T ♎	T ♎	S ♐	T ♑	F ♓	S ♈	W ♉	S ♋	M ♌	T ♎	S ♏
21.	T ♍	F ♎	F ♏	M ♐	W ♒	S ♓	M ♈	T ♊	S ♋	T ♌	F ♎	S ♏
22.	W ♍	S ♏	S ♏	T ♑	T ♒	S ♈	T ♉	F ♊	M ♌	W ♍	S ♏	M ♐
23.	T ♎	S ♏	S ♐	W ♑	F ♓	M ♈	W ♉	S ♋	T ♌	T ♍	S ♐	T ♑
24.	F ♎	M ♐	M ♐	T ♒	S ♓	T ♈	T ♊	S ♋	W ♍	F ♎	M ♐	W ♑
25.	S ♎	T ♐	T ♑	F ♒	S ♓	W ♉	F ♊	M ♋	T ♍	S ♏	T ♐	T ♑
26.	S ♏	W ♑	W ♑	S ♓	M ♈	T ♉	S ♊	T ♌	F ♎	S ♏	W ♑	F ♒
27.	M ♏	T ♑	T ♑	S ♓	T ♈	F ♊	S ♋	W ♍	S ♎	M ♏	T ♑	S ♒
28.	T ♐	F ♒	F ♒	M ♓	W ♉	S ♊	M ♋	T ♍	S ♏	T ♐	F ♒	S ♓
29.	W ♐		S ♒	T ♈	T ♉	S ♋	T ♌	F ♍	M ♏	W ♐	S ♒	M ♓
30.	T ♑		S ♓	W ♈	F ♉	M ♋	W ♌	S ♎	T ♏	T ♑	S ♒	T ♈
31.	F ♑		M ♓		S ♊		T ♌	S ♎		F ♑		W ♈

2004

January	February	March	April	May	June	July	August	September	October	November	December	
T	S	M	T	S	T	T	S	W	F	M	W	1.
F	M	T	F	S	W	F	M	T	S	T	T	2.
S	T	W	S	M	T	S	T	F	S	W	F	3.
S	W	T	S	T	F	S	W	S	M	T	S	4.
M	T	F	M	W	S	M	T	S	T	F	S	5.
T	F	S	T	T	S	T	F	M	W	S	M	6.
W	S	S	W	F	M	W	S	T	T	S	T	7.
T	S	M	T	S	T	T	S	W	F	M	W	8.
F	M	T	F	S	W	F	M	T	S	T	T	9.
S	T	W	S	M	T	S	T	F	S	W	F	10.
S	W	T	S	T	F	S	W	S	M	T	S	11.
M	T	F	M	W	S	M	T	S	T	F	S	12.
T	F	S	T	T	S	T	F	M	W	S	M	13.
W	S	S	W	F	M	W	S	T	T	S	T	14.
T	S	M	T	S	T	T	S	W	F	M	W	15.
F	M	T	F	S	W	F	M	T	S	T	T	16.
S	T	W	S	M	T	S	T	F	S	W	F	17.
S	W	T	S	T	F	S	W	S	M	T	S	18.
M	T	F	M	W	S	M	T	S	T	F	S	19.
T	F	S	T	T	S	T	F	M	W	S	M	20.
W	S	S	W	F	M	W	S	T	T	S	T	21.
T	S	M	T	S	T	T	S	W	F	M	W	22.
F	M	T	F	S	W	F	M	T	S	T	T	23.
S	T	W	S	M	T	S	T	F	S	W	F	24.
S	W	T	S	T	F	S	W	S	M	T	S	25.
M	T	F	M	W	S	M	T	S	T	F	S	26.
T	F	S	T	T	S	T	F	M	W	S	M	27.
W	S	S	W	F	M	W	S	T	T	S	T	28.
T	S	M	T	S	T	T	S	W	F	M	W	29.
F		T	F	S	W	F	M	T	S	T	T	30.
S		W		M		S	T		S		F	31.

2005

	January	February	March	April	May	June	July	August	September	October	November	December
1.	S ♍	T ♎	T ♏	F ♐	S ♒	W ♓	F ♉	M ♊	T ♌	S ♍	T ♎	T ♐
2.	S ♍	W ♏	W ♏	S ♑	M ♒	T ♈	S ♉	T ♋	F ♌	S ♍	W ♏	F ♐
3.	M ♎	T ♏	T ♐	S ♑	T ♓	F ♈	S ♊	W ♋	S ♍	M ♎	T ♏	S ♐
4.	T ♎	F ♐	F ♐	M ♒	W ♓	S ♉	M ♊	T ♋	S ♍	T ♎	F ♐	S ♑
5.	W ♏	S ♐	S ♑	T ♒	T ♈	S ♉	T ♊	F ♌	M ♍	W ♎	S ♐	M ♑
6.	T ♏	S ♑	S ♑	W ♓	F ♈	M ♊	W ♋	S ♌	T ♎	T ♏	S ♑	T ♒
7.	F ♏	M ♑	M ♒	T ♓	S ♈	T ♊	T ♋	S ♍	W ♎	F ♏	M ♑	W ♒
8.	S ♐	T ♒	T ♒	F ♈	S ♉	W ♊	F ♌	M ♍	T ♏	S ♐	T ♒	T ♓
9.	S ♐	W ♒	W ♒	S ♈	M ♉	T ♋	S ♌	T ♍	F ♏	S ♐	W ♒	F ♓
10.	M ♑	T ♓	T ♓	S ♉	T ♊	F ♋	S ♌	W ♎	S ♏	M ♑	T ♒	S ♈
11.	T ♑	F ♓	F ♓	M ♉	W ♊	S ♌	M ♍	T ♎	S ♐	T ♑	F ♓	S ♈
12.	W ♒	S ♈	S ♓	T ♊	T ♋	S ♌	T ♍	F ♏	M ♐	W ♒	S ♓	M ♉
13.	T ♒	S ♈	S ♈	W ♊	F ♋	M ♌	W ♎	S ♏	T ♑	T ♒	S ♈	T ♉
14.	F ♓	M ♉	M ♈	T ♊	S ♋	T ♍	T ♎	S ♐	W ♑	F ♓	M ♈	W ♊
15.	S ♓	T ♉	T ♉	F ♋	S ♌	W ♍	F ♎	M ♐	T ♒	S ♓	T ♉	T ♊
16.	S ♈	W ♉	W ♉	S ♋	M ♌	T ♎	S ♏	T ♑	F ♒	S ♈	W ♉	F ♊
17.	M ♈	T ♊	T ♊	S ♌	T ♍	F ♎	S ♏	W ♑	S ♓	M ♈	T ♊	S ♋
18.	T ♉	F ♊	F ♊	M ♌	W ♍	S ♏	M ♐	T ♒	S ♓	T ♉	F ♊	S ♋
19.	W ♉	S ♋	S ♋	T ♌	T ♍	S ♏	T ♐	F ♒	M ♈	W ♉	S ♋	M ♌
20.	T ♊	S ♋	S ♋	W ♍	F ♎	M ♏	W ♑	S ♓	T ♈	T ♉	S ♋	T ♌
21.	F ♊	M ♋	M ♌	T ♍	S ♎	T ♐	T ♑	S ♓	W ♈	F ♊	M ♋	W ♌
22.	S ♊	T ♌	T ♌	F ♎	S ♏	W ♑	F ♒	M ♈	T ♉	S ♊	T ♌	T ♍
23.	S ♋	W ♌	W ♌	S ♎	M ♐	T ♑	S ♒	T ♈	F ♊	S ♋	W ♌	F ♍
24.	M ♋	T ♍	T ♍	S ♏	T ♐	F ♑	S ♓	W ♈	S ♊	M ♋	T ♍	S ♎
25.	T ♌	F ♍	F ♎	M ♏	W ♐	S ♒	M ♓	T ♉	S ♊	T ♌	F ♍	S ♎
26.	W ♌	S ♍	S ♎	T ♏	T ♑	S ♒	T ♈	F ♉	M ♋	W ♌	S ♍	M ♎
27.	T ♌	S ♎	S ♎	W ♐	F ♑	M ♓	W ♈	S ♊	T ♋	T ♌	S ♎	T ♏
28.	F ♍	M ♎	M ♏	T ♐	S ♒	T ♓	T ♉	S ♊	W ♌	F ♍	M ♎	W ♏
29.	S ♍		T ♏	F ♑	S ♒	W ♈	F ♉	M ♋	T ♌	S ♍	T ♏	T ♐
30.	S ♎		W ♐	S ♑	M ♓	T ♈	S ♉	T ♋	F ♌	S ♎	W ♏	F ♐
31.	M ♎		T ♐		T ♓		S ♊	W ♋		M ♎		S ♑

2006

	January	February	March	April	May	June	July	August	September	October	November	December
1.	S ♑	W ♓	W ♓	S ♉	M ♊	T ♌	S ♍	T ♎	F ♐	S ♑	W ♓	F ♈
2.	M ♒	T ♈	T ♈	S ♊	T ♋	F ♌	S ♍	W ♏	S ♐	M ♑	T ♓	S ♈
3.	T ♒	F ♈	F ♈	M ♊	W ♋	S ♍	M ♎	T ♏	S ♑	T ♒	F ♈	S ♉
4.	W ♓	S ♈	S ♉	T ♊	T ♋	S ♍	T ♎	F ♐	M ♑	W ♒	S ♈	M ♉
5.	T ♓	S ♉	S ♉	W ♋	F ♌	M ♍	W ♎	S ♐	T ♒	T ♓	S ♉	T ♊
6.	F ♈	M ♉	M ♊	T ♋	S ♌	T ♎	T ♏	S ♐	W ♒	F ♓	M ♉	W ♊
7.	S ♈	T ♊	T ♊	F ♌	S ♍	W ♎	F ♏	M ♑	T ♓	S ♈	T ♊	T ♋
8.	S ♉	W ♊	W ♋	S ♌	M ♍	T ♏	S ♐	T ♑	F ♓	S ♈	W ♊	F ♋
9.	M ♉	T ♋	T ♋	S ♌	T ♍	F ♏	S ♐	W ♒	S ♈	M ♉	T ♋	S ♌
10.	T ♉	F ♋	F ♋	M ♍	W ♎	S ♏	M ♑	T ♒	S ♈	T ♉	F ♋	S ♌
11.	W ♊	S ♋	S ♌	T ♍	T ♎	S ♐	T ♑	F ♓	M ♉	W ♊	S ♋	M ♍
12.	T ♊	S ♌	S ♌	W ♎	F ♏	M ♐	W ♒	S ♓	T ♉	T ♊	S ♌	T ♍
13.	F ♋	M ♌	M ♍	T ♎	S ♏	T ♑	T ♒	S ♈	W ♊	F ♋	M ♌	W ♍
14.	S ♋	T ♍	T ♍	F ♎	S ♐	W ♑	F ♓	M ♈	T ♊	S ♋	T ♍	T ♎
15.	S ♌	W ♍	W ♍	S ♏	M ♐	T ♒	S ♓	T ♉	F ♊	S ♌	W ♍	F ♎
16.	M ♌	T ♍	T ♎	S ♏	T ♐	F ♒	S ♓	W ♉	S ♋	M ♌	T ♍	S ♏
17.	T ♌	F ♎	F ♎	M ♐	W ♑	S ♓	M ♈	T ♊	S ♋	T ♌	F ♎	S ♏
18.	W ♍	S ♎	S ♏	T ♐	T ♑	S ♓	T ♈	F ♊	M ♌	W ♍	S ♎	M ♏
19.	T ♍	S ♏	S ♏	W ♑	F ♒	M ♈	W ♉	S ♋	T ♌	T ♍	S ♏	T ♐
20.	F ♎	M ♏	M ♏	T ♑	S ♒	T ♈	T ♉	S ♋	W ♌	F ♎	M ♏	W ♐
21.	S ♎	T ♏	T ♐	F ♑	S ♓	W ♉	F ♊	M ♋	T ♍	S ♎	T ♏	T ♑
22.	S ♎	W ♐	W ♐	S ♒	M ♓	T ♉	S ♊	T ♌	F ♍	S ♎	W ♐	F ♑
23.	M ♏	T ♐	T ♑	S ♒	T ♈	F ♉	S ♋	W ♍	S ♎	M ♏	T ♐	S ♒
24.	T ♏	F ♑	F ♑	M ♓	W ♈	S ♊	M ♋	T ♍	S ♎	T ♏	F ♑	S ♒
25.	W ♐	S ♑	S ♒	T ♓	T ♉	S ♋	T ♌	F ♍	M ♎	W ♐	S ♑	M ♒
26.	T ♐	S ♒	S ♒	W ♈	F ♉	M ♋	W ♌	S ♍	T ♏	T ♐	S ♒	T ♓
27.	F ♑	M ♒	M ♓	T ♉	S ♊	T ♋	T ♌	S ♎	W ♏	F ♐	M ♒	W ♓
28.	S ♑	T ♓	T ♓	F ♉	S ♊	W ♌	F ♍	M ♎	T ♐	S ♑	T ♓	T ♈
29.	S ♒		W ♈	S ♉	M ♊	T ♌	S ♍	T ♏	F ♐	S ♑	W ♓	F ♈
30.	M ♒		T ♈	S ♊	T ♋	F ♌	S ♍	W ♏	S ♑	M ♒	T ♈	S ♉
31.	T ♓		F ♉		W ♋		M ♎	T ♏		T ♒		S ♉

2007

	January	February	March	April	May	June	July	August	September	October	November	December
1.	M ♊	T ♋	T ♌	S ♍	T ♎	F ♐	S ♑	W ♓	S ♈	M ♊	T ♋	S ♍
2.	T ♊	F ♌	F ♌	M ♎	W ♏	S ♐	M ♑	T ♓	S ♉	T ♊	F ♌	S ♍
3.	W ♋	S ♌	S ♍	T ♎	T ♏	S ♑	T ♒	F ♈	M ♉	W ♋	S ♌	M ♍
4.	T ♋	S ♍	S ♍	W ♎	F ♐	M ♑	W ♒	S ♈	T ♊	T ♋	S ♍	T ♎
5.	F ♌	M ♍	M ♍	T ♏	S ♐	T ♒	T ♓	S ♉	W ♊	F ♌	M ♍	W ♎
6.	S ♌	T ♍	T ♎	F ♏	S ♐	W ♒	F ♓	M ♉	T ♋	S ♌	T ♎	T ♏
7.	S ♌	W ♎	W ♎	S ♐	M ♑	T ♒	S ♈	T ♉	F ♋	S ♌	W ♎	F ♏
8.	M ♍	T ♎	T ♏	S ♐	T ♑	F ♓	S ♈	W ♊	S ♌	M ♍	T ♎	S ♏
9.	T ♍	F ♏	F ♏	M ♐	W ♒	S ♓	M ♉	T ♊	S ♌	T ♍	F ♏	S ♐
10.	W ♎	S ♏	S ♏	T ♑	T ♒	S ♈	T ♉	F ♋	M ♌	W ♎	S ♏	M ♐
11.	T ♎	S ♏	S ♐	W ♑	F ♓	M ♈	W ♊	S ♋	T ♍	T ♎	S ♏	T ♑
12.	F ♎	M ♐	M ♐	T ♒	S ♓	T ♉	T ♊	S ♌	W ♍	F ♎	M ♐	W ♑
13.	S ♏	T ♐	T ♑	F ♒	S ♓	W ♉	F ♋	M ♌	T ♎	S ♏	T ♐	T ♑
14.	S ♏	W ♑	W ♑	S ♓	M ♈	T ♊	S ♋	T ♍	F ♎	S ♏	W ♑	F ♒
15.	M ♐	T ♑	T ♑	S ♓	T ♈	F ♊	S ♋	W ♍	S ♏	M ♐	T ♑	S ♒
16.	T ♐	F ♒	F ♒	M ♈	W ♉	S ♋	M ♌	T ♍	S ♏	T ♐	F ♒	S ♓
17.	W ♐	S ♒	S ♒	T ♈	T ♉	S ♋	T ♌	F ♎	M ♏	W ♐	S ♒	M ♓
18.	T ♑	S ♓	S ♓	W ♉	F ♊	M ♌	W ♍	S ♎	T ♐	T ♑	S ♒	T ♈
19.	F ♑	M ♓	M ♓	T ♉	S ♊	T ♌	T ♍	S ♏	W ♐	F ♑	M ♓	W ♈
20.	S ♒	T ♈	T ♈	F ♊	S ♋	W ♌	F ♎	M ♏	T ♑	S ♒	T ♓	T ♉
21.	S ♒	W ♈	W ♈	S ♊	M ♋	T ♍	S ♎	T ♏	F ♑	S ♒	W ♈	F ♉
22.	M ♓	T ♉	T ♉	S ♋	T ♌	F ♍	S ♎	W ♐	S ♑	M ♓	T ♈	S ♊
23.	T ♓	F ♉	F ♉	M ♋	W ♌	S ♎	M ♏	T ♐	S ♒	T ♓	F ♉	S ♊
24.	W ♈	S ♊	S ♊	T ♌	T ♍	S ♎	T ♏	F ♑	M ♒	W ♓	S ♊	M ♋
25.	T ♈	S ♊	S ♊	W ♌	F ♍	M ♎	W ♐	S ♑	T ♓	T ♈	S ♊	T ♋
26.	F ♉	M ♊	M ♋	T ♌	S ♍	T ♏	T ♐	S ♒	W ♈	F ♉	M ♊	W ♌
27.	S ♉	T ♋	T ♋	F ♍	S ♎	W ♏	F ♐	M ♒	T ♈	S ♉	T ♋	T ♌
28.	S ♊	W ♋	W ♌	S ♍	M ♎	T ♐	S ♑	T ♓	F ♈	S ♉	W ♋	F ♌
29.	M ♊		T ♌	S ♎	T ♏	F ♐	S ♑	W ♓	S ♉	M ♊	T ♌	S ♍
30.	T ♋		F ♌	M ♎	W ♏	S ♑	M ♒	T ♓	S ♉	T ♊	F ♌	S ♍
31.	W ♋		S ♍		T ♏		T ♒	F ♈		W ♋		M ♎

2008

January	February	March	April	May	June	July	August	September	October	November	December	
T ♎	F ♐	S ♐	T ♒	T ♓	S ♉	T ♊	F ♌	M ♍	W ♎	S ♐	M ♑	1.
W ♎	S ♐	S ♑	W ♒	F ♌	M ♉	W ♊	S ♌	T ♎	T ♏	S ♐	T ♑	2.
T ♏	S ♐	M ♑	T ♓	S ♈	T ♊	T ♋	S ♍	W ♎	F ♏	M ♑	W ♒	3.
F ♏	M ♑	T ♑	F ♓	S ♈	W ♊	F ♋	M ♍	T ♏	S ♐	T ♑	T ♒	4.
S ♐	T ♑	W ♒	S ♓	M ♉	T ♋	S ♌	T ♍	F ♏	S ♐	W ♑	F ♓	5.
S ♐	W ♒	T ♒	S ♈	T ♉	F ♋	S ♌	W ♎	S ♏	M ♐	T ♒	S ♓	6.
M ♐	T ♒	F ♓	M ♈	W ♊	S ♌	M ♍	T ♎	S ♐	T ♑	F ♒	S ♓	7.
T ♑	F ♒	S ♓	T ♉	T ♊	S ♌	T ♍	F ♏	M ♐	W ♑	S ♓	M ♈	8.
W ♑	S ♓	S ♈	W ♉	F ♋	M ♌	W ♎	S ♏	T ♑	T ♒	S ♓	T ♈	9.
T ♒	S ♓	M ♈	T ♊	S ♋	T ♍	T ♎	S ♐	W ♑	F ♒	M ♈	W ♉	10.
F ♒	M ♈	T ♉	F ♊	S ♌	W ♍	F ♎	M ♐	T ♑	S ♒	T ♈	T ♉	11.
S ♓	T ♈	W ♉	S ♋	M ♌	T ♎	S ♏	T ♐	F ♒	S ♓	W ♉	F ♊	12.
S ♓	W ♉	T ♊	S ♋	T ♍	F ♎	S ♏	W ♑	S ♒	M ♓	T ♉	S ♊	13.
M ♓	T ♉	F ♊	M ♌	W ♍	S ♏	M ♐	T ♑	S ♓	T ♈	F ♊	S ♋	14.
T ♈	F ♊	S ♋	T ♌	T ♍	S ♏	T ♐	F ♒	M ♓	W ♈	S ♊	M ♋	15.
W ♈	S ♊	S ♋	W ♍	F ♎	M ♏	W ♐	S ♒	T ♈	T ♉	S ♋	T ♌	16.
T ♉	S ♋	M ♋	T ♍	S ♎	T ♐	T ♑	S ♒	W ♈	F ♉	M ♋	W ♌	17.
F ♉	M ♋	T ♌	F ♎	S ♏	W ♐	F ♑	M ♓	T ♈	S ♊	T ♌	T ♍	18.
S ♊	T ♌	W ♌	S ♎	M ♏	T ♑	S ♒	T ♓	F ♉	S ♊	W ♌	F ♍	19.
S ♊	W ♌	T ♍	S ♏	T ♏	F ♑	S ♒	W ♈	S ♉	M ♋	T ♌	S ♎	20.
M ♋	T ♍	F ♍	M ♏	W ♐	S ♑	M ♒	T ♈	S ♊	T ♋	F ♍	S ♎	21.
T ♌	F ♍	S ♎	T ♏	T ♐	S ♒	T ♓	F ♉	M ♊	W ♌	S ♍	M ♏	22.
W ♌	S ♍	S ♎	W ♐	F ♑	M ♒	W ♓	S ♉	T ♋	T ♌	S ♎	T ♏	23.
T ♌	S ♎	M ♎	T ♐	S ♑	T ♓	T ♈	S ♊	W ♋	F ♍	M ♎	W ♏	24.
F ♍	M ♎	T ♏	F ♐	S ♑	W ♓	F ♈	M ♊	T ♌	S ♍	T ♏	T ♐	25.
S ♍	T ♏	W ♏	S ♑	M ♒	T ♓	S ♉	T ♊	F ♌	S ♍	W ♏	F ♐	26.
S ♎	W ♏	T ♐	S ♑	T ♒	F ♈	S ♉	W ♋	S ♍	M ♎	T ♐	S ♑	27.
M ♎	T ♏	F ♐	M ♒	W ♓	S ♈	M ♊	T ♋	S ♍	T ♏	F ♐	S ♑	28.
T ♎	F ♐	S ♐	T ♒	T ♓	S ♉	T ♊	F ♌	M ♎	W ♏	S ♐	M ♑	29.
W ♏		S ♑	W ♒	F ♈	M ♉	W ♋	S ♍	T ♎	T ♏	S ♑	T ♒	30.
T ♏		M ♑		S ♈		T ♋	S ♍		F ♐		W ♒	31.

2009

	January	February	March	April	May	June	July	August	September	October	November	December
1.	T ♒	S ♈	S ♈	W ♊	F ♋	M ♍	W ♎	S ♐	T ♑	T ♓	S ♈	T ♉
2.	F ♓	M ♉	M ♉	T ♋	S ♌	T ♎	T ♏	S ♐	W ♒	F ♓	M ♉	W ♊
3.	S ♓	T ♉	T ♉	F ♋	S ♌	W ♎	F ♏	M ♑	T ♒	S ♓	T ♉	T ♊
4.	S ♈	W ♉	W ♊	S ♌	M ♍	T ♏	S ♐	T ♑	F ♓	S ♈	W ♉	F ♋
5.	M ♈	T ♊	T ♊	S ♌	T ♍	F ♏	S ♐	W ♒	S ♓	M ♈	T ♊	S ♋
6.	T ♉	F ♊	F ♋	M ♍	W ♎	S ♏	M ♐	T ♒	S ♈	T ♉	F ♊	S ♌
7.	W ♉	S ♋	S ♋	T ♍	T ♎	S ♐	T ♑	F ♒	M ♈	W ♉	S ♋	M ♌
8.	T ♊	S ♋	S ♌	W ♍	F ♏	M ♐	W ♑	S ♓	T ♈	T ♊	S ♋	T ♍
9.	F ♊	M ♌	M ♌	T ♎	S ♏	T ♑	T ♒	S ♓	W ♉	F ♊	M ♌	W ♍
10.	S ♋	T ♌	T ♍	F ♎	S ♏	W ♑	F ♒	M ♈	T ♉	S ♊	T ♌	T ♎
11.	S ♋	W ♍	W ♍	S ♏	M ♐	T ♑	S ♒	T ♈	F ♊	S ♋	W ♍	F ♎
12.	M ♌	T ♍	T ♎	S ♏	T ♐	F ♒	S ♓	W ♈	S ♊	M ♋	T ♍	S ♎
13.	T ♌	F ♎	F ♎	M ♐	W ♑	S ♒	M ♓	T ♉	S ♋	T ♌	F ♎	S ♏
14.	W ♍	S ♎	S ♎	T ♐	T ♑	S ♓	T ♈	F ♉	M ♋	W ♌	S ♎	M ♏
15.	T ♍	S ♏	S ♏	W ♐	F ♑	M ♓	W ♈	S ♊	T ♌	T ♍	S ♏	T ♐
16.	F ♎	M ♏	M ♏	T ♑	S ♒	T ♓	T ♉	S ♊	W ♌	F ♍	M ♏	W ♐
17.	S ♎	T ♏	T ♐	F ♑	S ♒	W ♈	F ♉	M ♋	T ♍	S ♎	T ♏	T ♑
18.	S ♎	W ♐	W ♐	S ♒	M ♓	T ♈	S ♉	T ♋	F ♍	S ♎	W ♐	F ♑
19.	M ♏	T ♐	T ♑	S ♒	T ♓	F ♉	S ♊	W ♌	S ♍	M ♏	T ♐	S ♑
20.	T ♏	F ♑	F ♑	M ♒	W ♈	S ♉	M ♊	T ♌	S ♎	T ♏	F ♑	S ♒
21.	W ♐	S ♑	S ♑	T ♓	T ♈	S ♊	T ♋	F ♍	M ♎	W ♐	S ♑	M ♒
22.	T ♐	S ♑	S ♒	W ♓	F ♈	M ♋	W ♋	S ♍	T ♏	T ♐	S ♑	T ♓
23.	F ♐	M ♒	M ♒	T ♈	S ♉	T ♋	T ♌	S ♎	W ♏	F ♐	M ♒	W ♓
24.	S ♑	T ♒	T ♓	F ♈	S ♊	W ♋	F ♌	M ♎	T ♐	S ♑	T ♒	T ♓
25.	S ♑	W ♓	W ♓	S ♈	M ♊	T ♌	S ♍	T ♏	F ♐	S ♑	W ♓	F ♈
26.	M ♒	T ♓	T ♈	S ♉	T ♊	F ♌	S ♍	W ♏	S ♑	M ♒	T ♓	S ♈
27.	T ♒	F ♈	F ♈	M ♊	W ♋	S ♍	M ♎	T ♏	S ♑	T ♒	F ♈	S ♉
28.	W ♒	S ♈	S ♈	T ♊	T ♋	S ♍	T ♎	F ♐	M ♑	W ♒	S ♈	M ♉
29.	T ♓		S ♉	W ♋	F ♌	M ♎	W ♏	S ♐	T ♒	T ♓	S ♈	T ♉
30.	F ♓		M ♉	T ♋	S ♌	T ♎	T ♏	S ♑	W ♒	F ♓	M ♉	W ♊
31.	S ♈		T ♊		S ♍		F ♐	M ♑		S ♈		T ♋

2010

January	February	March	April	May	June	July	August	September	October	November	December	
F ♋	M ♍	M ♍	T ♏	S ♐	T ♑	T ♒	S ♈	W ♉	F ♋	M ♌	W ♎	1.
S ♋	T ♍	T ♍	F ♏	S ♐	W ♒	F ♓	M ♈	T ♊	S ♋	T ♍	T ♎	2.
S ♌	W ♎	W ♎	S ♐	M ♑	T ♒	S ♓	T ♉	F ♊	S ♌	W ♍	F ♏	3.
M ♌	T ♎	T ♎	S ♐	T ♑	F ♓	S ♈	W ♉	S ♋	M ♌	T ♎	S ♏	4.
T ♍	F ♏	F ♏	M ♐	W ♒	S ♓	M ♈	T ♊	S ♋	T ♍	F ♎	S ♐	5.
W ♍	S ♏	S ♏	T ♑	T ♒	S ♈	T ♈	F ♊	M ♌	W ♍	S ♏	M ♐	6.
T ♎	S ♏	S ♐	W ♑	F ♒	M ♈	W ♉	S ♋	T ♌	T ♎	S ♏	T ♑	7.
F ♎	M ♐	M ♐	T ♒	S ♓	T ♈	T ♉	S ♋	W ♍	F ♎	M ♐	W ♑	8.
S ♏	T ♐	T ♑	F ♒	S ♓	W ♉	F ♊	M ♌	T ♍	S ♏	T ♐	T ♑	9.
S ♏	W ♑	W ♑	S ♒	M ♈	T ♉	S ♊	T ♌	F ♎	S ♏	W ♑	F ♒	10.
M ♐	T ♑	T ♑	S ♓	T ♈	F ♊	S ♋	W ♍	S ♎	M ♐	T ♑	S ♒	11.
T ♐	F ♒	F ♒	M ♓	W ♈	S ♊	M ♋	T ♍	S ♏	T ♐	F ♒	S ♓	12.
W ♐	S ♒	S ♒	T ♈	T ♉	S ♊	T ♌	F ♎	M ♏	W ♐	S ♒	M ♓	13.
T ♑	S ♒	S ♓	W ♈	F ♉	M ♋	W ♌	S ♎	T ♐	T ♑	S ♒	T ♓	14.
F ♑	M ♓	M ♓	T ♉	S ♊	T ♋	T ♍	S ♎	W ♐	F ♑	M ♓	W ♈	15.
S ♒	T ♓	T ♈	F ♉	S ♊	W ♌	F ♍	M ♏	T ♑	S ♒	T ♓	T ♈	16.
S ♒	W ♈	W ♈	S ♉	M ♋	T ♌	S ♎	T ♏	F ♑	S ♒	W ♈	F ♉	17.
M ♒	T ♈	T ♈	S ♊	T ♋	F ♍	S ♎	W ♐	S ♑	M ♒	T ♈	S ♉	18.
T ♓	F ♈	F ♉	M ♊	W ♌	S ♍	M ♏	T ♐	S ♒	T ♓	F ♈	S ♉	19.
W ♓	S ♉	S ♉	T ♋	T ♌	S ♎	T ♏	F ♑	M ♒	W ♓	S ♉	M ♊	20.
T ♈	S ♉	S ♉	W ♋	F ♍	M ♎	W ♐	S ♑	T ♓	T ♈	S ♉	T ♊	21.
F ♈	M ♊	M ♊	T ♌	S ♍	T ♏	T ♐	S ♑	W ♓	F ♈	M ♊	W ♋	22.
S ♈	T ♊	T ♊	F ♌	S ♍	W ♏	F ♐	M ♒	T ♈	S ♈	T ♊	T ♋	23.
S ♉	W ♋	W ♋	S ♍	M ♎	T ♐	S ♑	T ♓	F ♈	S ♉	W ♊	F ♌	24.
M ♉	T ♋	T ♋	S ♍	T ♎	F ♐	S ♑	W ♓	S ♈	M ♉	T ♋	S ♌	25.
T ♊	F ♋	F ♌	M ♎	W ♏	S ♑	M ♒	T ♓	S ♉	T ♊	F ♋	S ♍	26.
W ♊	S ♌	S ♌	T ♎	T ♐	S ♑	T ♒	F ♈	M ♉	W ♊	S ♌	M ♍	27.
T ♋	S ♍	S ♍	W ♏	F ♐	M ♑	W ♒	S ♈	T ♉	T ♋	S ♌	T ♎	28.
F ♋		M ♍	T ♏	S ♐	T ♒	T ♓	S ♈	W ♊	F ♋	M ♍	W ♎	29.
S ♌		T ♎	F ♏	S ♑	W ♒	F ♓	M ♉	T ♊	S ♋	T ♍	T ♏	30.
S ♌		W ♎		M ♑		S ♈	T ♉		S ♌		F ♏	31.

2011

	January	February	March	April	May	June	July	August	September	October	November	December
1.	S ♏	T ♑	T ♑	F ♓	S ♈	W ♊	F ♋	M ♌	T ♎	S ♏	T ♑	T ♒
2.	S ♐	W ♒	W ♒	S ♓	M ♈	T ♊	S ♋	T ♍	F ♏	S ♐	W ♒	F ♓
3.	M ♐	T ♒	T ♒	S ♈	T ♈	F ♊	S ♌	W ♍	S ♏	M ♐	T ♒	S ♓
4.	T ♑	F ♒	F ♓	M ♈	W ♉	S ♋	M ♌	T ♎	S ♐	T ♑	F ♒	S ♓
5.	W ♑	S ♓	S ♓	T ♉	T ♊	S ♋	T ♌	F ♎	M ♐	W ♑	S ♓	M ♈
6.	T ♒	S ♓	S ♓	W ♉	F ♊	M ♌	W ♍	S ♏	T ♐	T ♒	S ♓	T ♈
7.	F ♒	M ♈	M ♈	T ♉	S ♊	T ♌	T ♍	S ♏	W ♑	F ♒	M ♈	W ♉
8.	S ♒	T ♈	T ♈	F ♊	S ♋	W ♍	F ♎	M ♐	T ♑	S ♒	T ♈	T ♉
9.	S ♓	W ♈	W ♉	S ♊	M ♋	T ♍	S ♎	T ♐	F ♒	S ♓	W ♈	F ♉
10.	M ♓	T ♉	T ♉	S ♋	T ♌	F ♎	S ♏	W ♑	S ♒	M ♓	T ♉	S ♊
11.	T ♈	F ♉	F ♉	M ♋	W ♌	S ♎	M ♏	T ♑	S ♓	T ♈	F ♉	S ♊
12.	W ♈	S ♊	S ♊	T ♋	T ♍	S ♎	T ♐	F ♑	M ♓	W ♈	S ♊	M ♋
13.	T ♈	S ♊	S ♊	W ♌	F ♍	M ♏	W ♐	S ♒	T ♓	T ♈	S ♊	T ♋
14.	F ♉	M ♊	M ♋	T ♌	S ♎	T ♏	T ♑	S ♒	W ♈	F ♉	M ♊	W ♌
15.	S ♉	T ♋	T ♋	F ♍	S ♎	W ♐	F ♑	M ♓	T ♈	S ♉	T ♋	T ♌
16.	S ♊	W ♋	W ♌	S ♍	M ♏	T ♐	S ♒	T ♓	F ♉	S ♊	W ♋	F ♌
17.	M ♊	T ♌	T ♌	S ♎	T ♏	F ♑	S ♒	W ♈	S ♉	M ♊	T ♌	S ♍
18.	T ♋	F ♌	F ♍	M ♎	W ♐	S ♑	M ♒	T ♈	S ♉	T ♊	F ♌	S ♍
19.	W ♋	S ♍	S ♍	T ♏	T ♐	S ♒	T ♓	F ♈	M ♊	W ♋	S ♍	M ♎
20.	T ♌	S ♍	S ♎	W ♏	F ♑	M ♒	W ♓	S ♉	T ♊	T ♋	S ♍	T ♎
21.	F ♌	M ♎	M ♎	T ♐	S ♑	T ♓	T ♈	S ♉	W ♋	F ♌	M ♍	W ♏
22.	S ♍	T ♎	T ♏	F ♐	S ♑	W ♓	F ♈	M ♉	T ♋	S ♌	T ♎	T ♏
23.	S ♍	W ♏	W ♏	S ♑	M ♒	T ♓	S ♈	T ♊	F ♋	S ♍	W ♎	F ♐
24.	M ♎	T ♏	T ♐	S ♑	T ♒	F ♈	S ♉	W ♊	S ♌	M ♍	T ♏	S ♑
25.	T ♎	F ♐	F ♐	M ♒	W ♓	S ♈	M ♉	T ♋	S ♌	T ♎	F ♐	S ♑
26.	W ♎	S ♐	S ♐	T ♒	T ♓	S ♉	T ♊	F ♋	M ♍	W ♏	S ♐	M ♑
27.	T ♏	S ♑	S ♑	W ♒	F ♓	M ♉	W ♊	S ♌	T ♎	T ♏	S ♐	T ♒
28.	F ♏	M ♑	M ♑	T ♓	S ♈	T ♉	T ♊	S ♌	W ♎	F ♏	M ♑	W ♒
29.	S ♐		T ♒	F ♓	S ♈	W ♊	F ♋	M ♍	T ♎	S ♐	T ♑	T ♓
30.	S ♐		W ♒	S ♈	M ♉	T ♊	S ♌	T ♍	F ♏	S ♐	W ♒	F ♓
31.	M ♑		T ♓		T ♉		S ♌	W ♎		M ♑		S ♓

2012

January	February	March	April	May	June	July	August	September	October	November	December	
S ♈	W ♉	T ♊	S ♋	T ♍	F ♎	S ♐	W ♑	S ♓	M ♈	T ♊	S ♋	1.
M ♈	T ♊	F ♊	M ♌	W ♍	S ♏	M ♐	T ♒	S ♓	T ♉	F ♊	S ♋	2.
T ♉	F ♊	S ♋	T ♌	T ♍	S ♏	T ♑	F ♒	M ♈	W ♉	S ♊	M ♋	3.
W ♉	S ♊	S ♋	W ♍	F ♎	M ♐	W ♑	S ♓	T ♈	T ♉	S ♋	T ♌	4.
T ♉	S ♋	M ♌	T ♍	S ♎	T ♐	T ♑	S ♓	W ♉	F ♊	M ♋	W ♌	5.
F ♊	M ♋	T ♌	F ♎	S ♏	W ♑	F ♒	M ♈	T ♉	S ♊	T ♌	T ♍	6.
S ♊	T ♌	W ♌	S ♎	M ♏	T ♑	S ♒	T ♈	F ♉	S ♊	W ♌	F ♍	7.
S ♋	W ♌	T ♍	S ♏	T ♐	F ♒	S ♓	W ♈	S ♊	M ♋	T ♌	S ♎	8.
M ♋	T ♍	F ♍	M ♏	W ♐	S ♒	M ♓	T ♉	S ♊	T ♋	F ♍	S ♎	9.
T ♋	F ♍	S ♎	T ♐	T ♑	S ♓	T ♈	F ♉	M ♋	W ♌	S ♍	M ♏	10.
W ♌	S ♎	S ♎	W ♐	F ♑	M ♓	W ♈	S ♊	T ♋	T ♌	S ♎	T ♏	11.
T ♌	S ♎	M ♏	T ♑	S ♒	T ♓	T ♉	S ♊	W ♋	F ♍	M ♎	W ♐	12.
F ♍	M ♏	T ♏	F ♑	S ♒	W ♈	F ♉	M ♊	T ♌	S ♍	T ♏	T ♐	13.
S ♍	T ♏	W ♐	S ♒	M ♓	T ♈	S ♉	T ♋	F ♌	S ♎	W ♏	F ♑	14.
S ♎	W ♏	T ♐	S ♒	T ♓	F ♉	S ♊	W ♋	S ♍	M ♎	T ♐	S ♑	15.
M ♎	T ♐	F ♑	M ♒	W ♈	S ♉	M ♊	T ♌	S ♍	T ♎	F ♐	S ♒	16.
T ♏	F ♐	S ♑	T ♓	T ♈	S ♉	T ♊	F ♌	M ♎	W ♏	S ♑	M ♒	17.
W ♏	S ♑	S ♒	W ♓	F ♉	M ♊	W ♋	S ♌	T ♎	T ♏	S ♑	T ♒	18.
T ♐	S ♑	M ♒	T ♈	S ♉	T ♊	T ♋	S ♍	W ♏	F ♐	M ♒	W ♓	19.
F ♐	M ♒	T ♒	F ♈	S ♊	W ♋	F ♌	M ♍	T ♏	S ♐	T ♒	T ♓	20.
S ♑	T ♒	W ♓	S ♈	M ♊	T ♋	S ♌	T ♎	F ♐	S ♑	W ♓	F ♈	21.
S ♑	W ♓	T ♓	S ♉	T ♊	F ♋	S ♍	W ♎	S ♐	M ♑	T ♓	S ♈	22.
M ♒	T ♓	F ♈	M ♉	W ♊	S ♌	M ♍	T ♏	S ♑	T ♒	F ♓	S ♉	23.
T ♒	F ♓	S ♈	T ♊	T ♋	S ♌	T ♎	F ♏	M ♑	W ♒	S ♈	M ♉	24.
W ♒	S ♈	S ♉	W ♊	F ♋	M ♍	W ♎	S ♐	T ♒	T ♓	S ♈	T ♉	25.
T ♓	S ♈	M ♉	T ♊	S ♌	T ♍	T ♎	S ♐	W ♒	F ♓	M ♉	W ♊	26.
F ♓	M ♉	T ♉	F ♋	S ♌	W ♎	F ♏	M ♑	T ♒	S ♈	T ♉	T ♊	27.
S ♈	T ♉	W ♊	S ♋	M ♌	T ♎	S ♏	T ♑	F ♓	S ♈	W ♊	F ♋	28.
S ♈	W ♉	T ♊	S ♌	T ♍	F ♏	S ♐	W ♒	S ♓	M ♉	T ♊	S ♋	29.
M ♈		F ♋	M ♌	W ♍	S ♏	M ♐	T ♒	S ♈	T ♉	F ♊	S ♋	30.
T ♉		S ♋		T ♎		T ♑	F ♓		W ♉		M ♌	31.

2013

	January	February	March	April	May	June	July	August	September	October	November	December
1.	T ♌	F ♎	F ♎	M ♐	W ♑	S ♓	M ♈	T ♊	S ♋	T ♌	F ♎	S ♏
2.	W ♍	S ♎	S ♏	T ♐	T ♒	S ♓	T ♉	F ♊	M ♋	W ♍	S ♎	M ♏
3.	T ♍	S ♏	S ♏	W ♑	F ♒	M ♈	W ♉	S ♊	T ♌	T ♍	**S ♏**	**T ♐**
4.	F ♍	M ♏	M ♐	T ♑	S ♓	T ♈	T ♉	S ♋	W ♌	F ♍	M ♏	W ♐
5.	S ♎	T ♐	T ♐	F ♒	S ♓	W ♉	F ♊	M ♋	**T ♍**	**S ♎**	T ♐	T ♑
6.	S ♎	W ♐	W ♐	S ♒	M ♓	T ♉	S ♊	**T ♌**	F ♍	S ♎	W ♐	F ♑
7.	M ♏	T ♑	T ♑	S ♓	T ♈	F ♉	S ♋	W ♌	S ♎	M ♏	T ♑	S ♒
8.	T ♏	F ♑	F ♑	M ♓	W ♈	**S ♊**	**M ♋**	T ♌	S ♎	T ♏	F ♑	S ♒
9.	W ♐	S ♒	S ♒	T ♈	T ♉	S ♊	T ♋	F ♍	M ♎	W ♐	S ♒	M ♓
10.	T ♐	**S ♒**	S ♒	**W ♈**	**F ♉**	M ♋	W ♌	S ♍	T ♏	T ♐	S ♒	T ♓
11.	**F ♑**	M ♓	**M ♓**	T ♈	S ♊	T ♋	T ♌	S ♎	W ♏	F ♑	M ♒	W ♈
12.	S ♑	T ♓	T ♓	F ♉	S ♊	W ♋	F ♍	M ♎	T ♐	S ♑	T ♓	T ♈
13.	S ♒	W ♓	W ♈	S ♉	M ♊	T ♌	S ♍	T ♏	F ♐	S ♒	W ♓	F ♉
14.	M ♒	T ♈	T ♈	S ♊	T ♋	F ♌	S ♍	W ♏	S ♑	M ♒	T ♈	S ♉
15.	T ♓	F ♈	F ♉	M ♊	W ♋	S ♍	M ♎	T ♏	S ♑	T ♓	F ♈	S ♉
16.	W ♓	S ♉	S ♉	T ♊	T ♌	S ♍	T ♎	F ♐	M ♒	W ♓	S ♉	M ♊
17.	T ♈	S ♉	S ♉	W ♋	F ♌	M ♍	W ♏	S ♐	T ♒	T ♓	S ♉	T ♊
18.	F ♈	M ♊	M ♊	T ♋	S ♌	T ♎	T ♏	S ♑	W ♓	F ♈	M ♉	W ♋
19.	S ♈	T ♊	T ♊	F ♌	S ♍	W ♎	F ♐	M ♑	T ♓	S ♈	T ♊	T ♋
20.	S ♉	W ♊	W ♋	S ♌	M ♍	T ♏	S ♐	T ♒	F ♈	S ♉	W ♊	F ♋
21.	M ♉	T ♋	T ♋	S ♌	T ♎	F ♏	S ♑	W ♒	S ♈	M ♉	T ♋	S ♌
22.	T ♊	F ♋	F ♋	M ♍	W ♎	S ♐	M ♒	T ♓	S ♉	T ♊	F ♋	S ♌
23.	W ♊	S ♌	S ♌	T ♍	T ♏	S ♑	T ♒	F ♓	M ♉	W ♊	S ♌	M ♍
24.	T ♊	S ♌	S ♌	W ♎	F ♏	M ♑	W ♒	S ♈	T ♉	T ♊	S ♌	T ♍
25.	F ♋	M ♍	M ♍	T ♏	S ♐	T ♑	T ♓	S ♈	W ♊	F ♋	M ♌	W ♍
26.	S ♋	T ♍	T ♍	F ♏	S ♐	W ♒	F ♓	M ♉	T ♊	S ♋	T ♍	T ♎
27.	S ♌	W ♍	W ♎	S ♏	M ♑	T ♒	S ♈	T ♉	F ♋	S ♌	W ♍	F ♎
28.	M ♌	T ♎	T ♎	S ♐	T ♑	F ♓	S ♈	W ♊	S ♋	M ♌	T ♎	S ♏
29.	T ♍		F ♎	M ♐	W ♒	S ♓	M ♈	T ♊	S ♋	T ♌	F ♎	S ♏
30.	W ♍		S ♏	T ♑	T ♒	S ♈	T ♉	F ♊	M ♌	W ♍	S ♎	M ♐
31.	T ♍		S ♏		F ♒		W ♉	S ♋		T ♍		T ♐

2014

	January	February	March	April	May	June	July	August	September	October	November	December
1.	W ♑	S ♒	S ♓	T ♈	T ♊	S ♋	T ♌	F ♎	M ♏	W ♐	S ♒	M ♓
2.	T ♑	S ♓	S ♓	W ♉	F ♊	M ♋	W ♍	S ♎	T ♐	T ♑	S ♓	T ♈
3.	F ♒	M ♓	M ♈	T ♉	S ♊	T ♌	T ♍	S ♎	W ♐	F ♑	M ♓	W ♈
4.	S ♒	T ♈	T ♈	F ♊	S ♋	W ♌	F ♍	M ♏	T ♑	S ♒	T ♈	T ♉
5.	S ♓	W ♈	W ♉	S ♊	M ♋	T ♍	S ♎	T ♏	F ♑	S ♒	W ♈	F ♉
6.	M ♓	T ♉	T ♉	S ♋	T ♌	F ♍	S ♎	W ♐	S ♑	M ♓	T ♉	S ♊
7.	T ♈	F ♉	F ♉	M ♋	W ♌	S ♍	M ♏	T ♐	S ♒	T ♓	F ♉	S ♊
8.	W ♈	S ♊	S ♊	T ♌	T ♌	S ♎	T ♏	F ♑	M ♓	W ♈	S ♉	M ♋
9.	T ♈	S ♊	S ♊	W ♌	F ♍	M ♎	W ♏	S ♑	T ♓	T ♈	S ♊	T ♋
10.	F ♉	M ♊	M ♋	T ♍	S ♍	T ♏	T ♐	S ♒	W ♈	F ♉	M ♊	W ♋
11.	S ♉	T ♋	T ♋	F ♍	S ♎	W ♏	F ♐	M ♒	T ♈	S ♉	T ♋	T ♌
12.	S ♊	W ♋	W ♋	S ♍	M ♎	T ♐	S ♑	T ♓	F ♈	S ♊	W ♋	F ♌
13.	M ♊	T ♌	T ♌	S ♍	T ♎	F ♐	S ♑	W ♓	S ♉	M ♊	T ♌	S ♍
14.	T ♊	F ♌	F ♌	M ♎	W ♏	S ♑	M ♒	T ♈	S ♉	T ♋	F ♌	S ♍
15.	W ♋	S ♌	S ♍	T ♎	T ♏	S ♑	T ♒	F ♈	M ♊	W ♋	S ♌	M ♍
16.	T ♋	S ♍	S ♍	W ♏	F ♐	M ♒	W ♓	S ♉	T ♊	T ♋	S ♍	T ♎
17.	F ♌	M ♍	M ♍	T ♏	S ♐	T ♒	T ♓	S ♉	W ♋	F ♌	M ♍	W ♎
18.	S ♌	T ♎	T ♎	F ♐	S ♑	W ♓	F ♈	M ♊	T ♋	S ♌	T ♎	T ♏
19.	S ♌	W ♎	W ♎	S ♐	M ♑	T ♓	S ♈	T ♊	F ♋	S ♍	W ♎	F ♏
20.	M ♍	T ♎	T ♏	S ♐	T ♒	F ♈	S ♉	W ♊	S ♌	M ♍	T ♎	S ♐
21.	T ♍	F ♏	F ♏	M ♑	W ♒	S ♈	M ♉	T ♋	S ♌	T ♍	F ♏	S ♐
22.	W ♎	S ♏	S ♐	T ♑	T ♓	S ♈	T ♊	F ♋	M ♍	W ♎	S ♐	M ♑
23.	T ♎	S ♐	S ♐	W ♒	F ♓	M ♉	W ♊	S ♌	T ♍	T ♏	S ♐	T ♑
24.	F ♏	M ♐	M ♑	T ♒	S ♈	T ♉	T ♊	S ♌	W ♎	F ♎	M ♐	W ♑
25.	S ♏	T ♑	T ♑	F ♓	S ♈	W ♊	F ♋	M ♍	T ♎	S ♏	T ♑	T ♒
26.	S ♏	W ♑	W ♒	S ♓	M ♉	T ♊	S ♌	T ♍	F ♎	S ♏	W ♑	F ♒
27.	M ♐	T ♒	T ♒	S ♈	T ♉	F ♋	S ♌	W ♍	S ♏	M ♐	T ♒	S ♓
28.	T ♐	F ♒	F ♒	M ♈	W ♊	S ♋	M ♌	T ♎	S ♏	T ♐	F ♒	S ♓
29.	W ♑		S ♓	T ♉	T ♊	S ♋	T ♌	F ♎	M ♐	W ♑	S ♓	M ♈
30.	T ♒		S ♈	W ♉	F ♊	M ♌	W ♍	S ♎	T ♐	T ♑	S ♓	T ♈
31.	F ♒		M ♈		S ♋		T ♍	S ♏		F ♒		W ♉

2015

	January	February	March	April	May	June	July	August	September	October	November	December
1.	T ♉	S ♋	S ♋	W ♍	F ♎	M ♏	W ♐	S ♒	T ♈	T ♉	S ♋	T ♌
2.	F ♊	M ♋	M ♌	T ♍	S ♎	T ♐	T ♑	S ♓	W ♈	F ♊	M ♋	W ♌
3.	S ♊	T ♌	T ♌	F ♍	S ♎	W ♐	F ♑	M ♓	T ♉	S ♊	T ♌	T ♍
4.	S ♊	W ♌	W ♌	S ♎	M ♏	T ♐	S ♒	T ♈	F ♉	S ♊	W ♌	F ♍
5.	M ♋	T ♌	T ♍	S ♎	T ♏	F ♑	S ♒	W ♈	S ♊	M ♋	T ♌	S ♎
6.	T ♋	F ♍	F ♍	M ♏	W ♐	S ♑	M ♓	T ♈	S ♊	T ♋	F ♍	S ♎
7.	W ♌	S ♍	S ♍	T ♏	T ♐	S ♒	T ♓	F ♉	M ♋	W ♌	S ♍	M ♎
8.	T ♌	S ♎	S ♎	W ♏	F ♑	M ♒	W ♈	S ♉	T ♋	T ♌	S ♎	T ♏
9.	F ♍	M ♎	M ♎	T ♐	S ♑	T ♓	T ♈	S ♊	W ♋	F ♍	M ♎	W ♏
10.	S ♍	T ♎	T ♏	F ♐	S ♒	W ♓	F ♉	M ♊	T ♌	S ♍	T ♎	T ♐
11.	S ♍	W ♏	W ♏	S ♐	M ♒	T ♈	S ♉	T ♋	F ♌	S ♍	W ♏	F ♐
12.	M ♎	T ♏	T ♐	S ♑	T ♒	F ♈	S ♉	W ♋	S ♍	M ♎	T ♏	S ♐
13.	T ♎	F ♐	F ♐	M ♑	W ♓	S ♉	M ♊	T ♌	S ♍	T ♎	F ♐	S ♑
14.	W ♏	S ♐	S ♐	T ♒	T ♓	S ♉	T ♊	F ♌	M ♍	W ♏	S ♐	M ♑
15.	T ♏	S ♑	S ♑	W ♒	F ♈	M ♊	W ♋	S ♌	T ♎	T ♏	S ♐	T ♒
16.	F ♏	M ♑	M ♑	T ♓	S ♈	T ♊	T ♋	S ♍	W ♎	F ♏	M ♑	W ♒
17.	S ♐	T ♑	T ♒	F ♈	S ♉	W ♋	F ♌	M ♍	T ♏	S ♐	T ♑	T ♓
18.	S ♐	W ♓	W ♒	S ♈	M ♉	T ♋	S ♌	T ♎	F ♏	S ♐	W ♒	F ♓
19.	M ♑	T ♓	T ♓	S ♉	T ♊	F ♋	S ♌	W ♎	S ♏	M ♑	T ♒	S ♈
20.	T ♒	F ♓	F ♓	M ♉	W ♊	S ♌	M ♍	T ♎	S ♐	T ♑	F ♓	S ♈
21.	W ♒	S ♈	S ♈	T ♊	T ♋	S ♌	T ♍	F ♏	M ♐	W ♑	S ♓	M ♈
22.	T ♒	S ♈	S ♈	W ♊	F ♋	M ♍	W ♎	S ♏	T ♑	T ♒	S ♈	T ♉
23.	F ♓	M ♈	M ♉	T ♊	S ♌	T ♍	T ♎	S ♐	W ♑	F ♒	M ♈	W ♉
24.	S ♓	T ♉	T ♉	F ♋	S ♌	W ♍	F ♎	M ♐	T ♒	S ♓	T ♉	T ♊
25.	S ♈	W ♉	W ♊	S ♋	M ♌	T ♎	S ♏	T ♐	F ♒	S ♓	W ♊	F ♊
26.	M ♈	T ♊	T ♊	S ♌	T ♍	F ♎	S ♏	W ♑	S ♓	M ♈	T ♊	S ♋
27.	T ♉	F ♊	F ♋	M ♌	W ♍	S ♏	M ♐	T ♑	S ♓	T ♉	F ♊	S ♋
28.	W ♉	S ♋	S ♋	T ♌	T ♎	S ♏	T ♐	F ♒	M ♈	W ♉	S ♋	M ♌
29.	T ♊		S ♋	W ♍	F ♎	M ♏	W ♑	S ♓	T ♈	T ♉	S ♋	T ♌
30.	F ♊		M ♌	T ♍	S ♎	T ♐	T ♑	S ♓	W ♉	F ♊	M ♋	W ♍
31.	S ♊		T ♌		S ♏		F ♒	M ♓		S ♊		T ♍

2016

January	February	March	April	May	June	July	August	September	October	November	December	
F ♍	M ♏	T ♐	F ♑	S ♒	W ♈	F ♉	M ♋	T ♍	S ♎	T ♏	T ♐	1.
S ♎	T ♏	W ♐	S ♑	M ♓	T ♈	S ♊	T ♌	F ♍	S ♎	W ♐	F ♑	2.
S ♎	W ♐	T ♐	S ♒	T ♓	F ♉	S ♊	W ♌	S ♍	M ♏	T ♐	S ♑	3.
M ♏	T ♐	F ♑	M ♒	W ♈	S ♉	M ♋	T ♌	S ♎	T ♏	F ♐	S ♒	4.
T ♏	F ♐	S ♑	T ♓	T ♈	S ♊	T ♋	F ♍	M ♎	W ♏	S ♑	M ♒	5.
W ♏	S ♑	S ♒	W ♓	F ♉	M ♊	W ♌	S ♍	T ♏	T ♐	S ♑	T ♒	6.
T ♐	S ♑	M ♒	T ♈	S ♉	T ♋	T ♌	S ♎	W ♏	F ♐	M ♒	W ♓	7.
F ♐	M ♒	T ♓	F ♈	S ♊	W ♋	F ♍	M ♎	T ♏	S ♑	T ♒	T ♈	8.
S ♑	T ♒	W ♓	S ♉	M ♊	T ♌	S ♍	T ♎	F ♐	S ♑	W ♓	F ♈	9.
S ♑	W ♓	T ♈	S ♉	T ♋	F ♌	S ♍	W ♏	S ♐	M ♑	T ♓	S ♈	10.
M ♒	T ♓	F ♈	M ♊	W ♋	S ♍	M ♎	T ♏	S ♑	T ♒	F ♈	S ♉	11.
T ♒	F ♈	S ♉	T ♊	T ♌	S ♍	T ♎	F ♐	M ♑	W ♒	S ♈	M ♉	12.
W ♓	S ♈	S ♉	W ♋	F ♌	M ♍	W ♏	S ♐	T ♒	T ♓	S ♈	T ♊	13.
T ♓	S ♉	M ♊	T ♋	S ♌	T ♎	T ♏	S ♐	W ♒	F ♓	M ♉	W ♊	14.
F ♓	M ♉	T ♊	F ♌	S ♍	W ♎	F ♏	M ♑	T ♒	S ♈	T ♉	T ♋	15.
S ♈	T ♊	W ♊	S ♌	M ♍	T ♏	S ♐	T ♑	F ♓	S ♈	W ♊	F ♋	16.
S ♈	W ♊	T ♋	S ♍	T ♎	F ♏	S ♐	W ♒	S ♈	M ♉	T ♊	S ♌	17.
M ♉	T ♋	F ♋	M ♍	W ♎	S ♏	M ♑	T ♒	S ♈	T ♉	F ♋	S ♌	18.
T ♉	F ♋	S ♌	T ♍	T ♎	S ♐	T ♑	F ♓	M ♈	W ♊	S ♋	M ♍	19.
W ♊	S ♋	S ♌	W ♎	F ♏	M ♐	W ♑	S ♓	T ♉	T ♊	S ♌	T ♍	20.
T ♊	S ♌	M ♍	T ♎	S ♏	T ♑	T ♒	S ♈	W ♉	F ♋	M ♌	W ♍	21.
F ♋	M ♍	T ♍	F ♎	S ♐	W ♑	F ♒	M ♈	T ♊	S ♋	T ♍	T ♎	22.
S ♋	T ♍	W ♎	S ♏	M ♐	T ♒	S ♓	T ♉	F ♊	S ♌	W ♍	F ♎	23.
S ♌	W ♍	T ♎	S ♏	T ♐	F ♒	S ♓	W ♉	S ♋	M ♌	T ♎	S ♏	24.
M ♌	T ♎	F ♎	M ♐	W ♑	S ♒	M ♈	T ♊	S ♋	T ♌	F ♎	S ♏	25.
T ♌	F ♎	S ♏	T ♐	T ♑	S ♓	T ♈	F ♊	M ♌	W ♍	S ♎	M ♏	26.
W ♍	S ♎	S ♏	W ♑	F ♒	M ♓	W ♉	S ♊	T ♌	T ♍	S ♏	T ♐	27.
T ♍	S ♏	M ♏	T ♑	S ♒	T ♈	T ♉	S ♋	W ♍	F ♎	M ♏	W ♐	28.
F ♎	M ♏	T ♐	F ♑	S ♓	W ♈	F ♊	M ♋	T ♍	S ♎	T ♐	T ♑	29.
S ♎		W ♐	S ♒	M ♓	T ♉	S ♊	T ♌	F ♍	S ♎	W ♐	F ♑	30.
S ♎		T ♑		T ♈		S ♋	W ♌		M ♏		S ♑	31.

2017

	January	February	March	April	May	June	July	August	September	October	November	December
1.	S ♒	W ♈	W ♈	S ♊	M ♋	T ♍	S ♎	T ♏	F ♑	S ♒	W ♈	F ♉
2.	M ♒	T ♈	T ♈	S ♊	T ♋	F ♍	S ♎	W ♐	S ♑	M ♒	T ♈	S ♉
3.	T ♓	F ♈	F ♉	M ♋	W ♌	S ♍	M ♏	T ♐	S ♒	T ♓	F ♈	S ♊
4.	W ♓	S ♉	S ♉	T ♋	T ♌	S ♎	T ♏	F ♐	M ♒	W ♓	S ♉	M ♊
5.	T ♈	S ♉	S ♊	W ♌	F ♍	M ♎	W ♏	S ♑	T ♒	T ♈	S ♉	T ♋
6.	F ♈	M ♊	M ♊	T ♌	S ♍	T ♏	T ♐	S ♑	W ♓	F ♈	M ♊	W ♋
7.	S ♉	T ♊	T ♋	F ♌	S ♎	W ♏	F ♐	M ♒	T ♓	S ♉	T ♊	T ♌
8.	S ♉	W ♋	W ♋	S ♍	M ♎	T ♐	S ♑	T ♒	F ♈	S ♉	W ♋	F ♌
9.	M ♊	T ♋	T ♌	S ♍	T ♎	F ♐	S ♑	W ♓	S ♈	M ♉	T ♋	S ♍
10.	T ♊	F ♌	F ♌	M ♎	W ♏	S ♐	M ♑	T ♓	S ♉	T ♊	F ♌	S ♍
11.	W ♋	S ♌	S ♍	T ♎	T ♏	S ♑	T ♒	F ♈	M ♉	W ♊	S ♌	M ♍
12.	T ♋	S ♍	S ♍	W ♏	F ♐	M ♑	W ♒	S ♈	T ♊	T ♋	S ♍	T ♎
13.	F ♋	M ♍	M ♍	T ♏	S ♐	T ♒	T ♓	S ♈	W ♊	F ♋	M ♍	W ♎
14.	S ♌	T ♎	T ♎	F ♏	S ♐	W ♒	F ♓	M ♉	T ♋	S ♌	T ♎	T ♏
15.	S ♌	W ♎	W ♎	S ♐	M ♑	T ♒	S ♈	T ♉	F ♋	S ♌	W ♎	F ♏
16.	M ♍	T ♎	T ♏	S ♐	T ♑	F ♓	S ♈	W ♊	S ♋	M ♍	T ♎	S ♏
17.	T ♍	F ♏	F ♏	M ♑	W ♒	S ♓	M ♈	T ♊	S ♌	T ♍	F ♏	S ♐
18.	W ♎	S ♏	S ♏	T ♑	T ♒	S ♈	T ♉	F ♋	M ♌	W ♎	S ♏	M ♐
19.	T ♎	S ♐	S ♐	W ♑	F ♒	M ♈	W ♉	S ♋	T ♍	T ♎	S ♐	T ♑
20.	F ♏	M ♐	M ♐	T ♒	S ♓	T ♉	T ♊	S ♌	W ♍	F ♎	M ♐	W ♑
21.	S ♏	T ♑	T ♑	F ♒	S ♈	W ♉	F ♊	M ♌	T ♎	S ♏	T ♐	T ♑
22.	S ♏	W ♑	W ♑	S ♓	M ♈	T ♊	S ♋	T ♍	F ♎	S ♏	W ♑	F ♒
23.	M ♐	T ♑	T ♑	S ♓	T ♈	F ♊	S ♋	W ♍	S ♏	M ♐	T ♑	S ♒
24.	T ♐	F ♒	F ♒	M ♈	W ♉	S ♋	M ♌	T ♍	S ♏	T ♐	F ♒	S ♓
25.	W ♑	S ♒	S ♒	T ♈	T ♊	S ♋	T ♌	F ♎	M ♏	W ♐	S ♒	M ♓
26.	T ♑	S ♓	S ♓	W ♈	F ♊	M ♌	W ♍	S ♎	T ♐	T ♑	S ♒	T ♈
27.	F ♑	M ♓	M ♓	T ♉	S ♊	T ♌	T ♍	S ♏	W ♐	F ♑	M ♓	W ♈
28.	S ♒	T ♈	T ♈	F ♉	S ♋	W ♌	F ♎	M ♏	T ♑	S ♒	T ♓	T ♈
29.	S ♒		W ♈	S ♉	M ♋	T ♍	S ♎	T ♐	F ♑	S ♒	W ♈	F ♉
30.	M ♓		T ♉	S ♊	T ♌	F ♍	S ♎	W ♐	S ♑	M ♓	T ♈	S ♉
31.	T ♓		F ♉		W ♌		M ♏	T ♐		T ♓		S ♊

2018

January	February	March	April	May	June	July	August	September	October	November	December	
M ♊	T ♌	T ♌	S ♎	T ♏	F ♑	S ♒	W ♓	S ♉	M ♊	T ♌	S ♍	1.
T ♋	F ♍	F ♍	M ♏	W ♐	S ♑	M ♒	T ♈	S ♉	T ♋	F ♌	S ♎	2.
W ♋	S ♍	S ♍	T ♏	T ♐	S ♒	T ♓	F ♈	M ♊	W ♋	S ♍	M ♎	3.
T ♌	S ♎	S ♎	W ♏	F ♐	M ♒	W ♓	S ♈	T ♊	T ♌	S ♍	T ♏	4.
F ♌	M ♎	M ♎	T ♐	S ♑	T ♒	T ♈	S ♉	W ♋	F ♌	M ♎	W ♏	5.
S ♍	T ♎	T ♏	F ♐	S ♑	W ♓	F ♈	M ♉	T ♋	S ♍	T ♎	T ♏	6.
S ♍	W ♏	W ♏	S ♑	M ♒	T ♓	S ♈	T ♊	F ♌	S ♍	W ♏	F ♐	7.
M ♎	T ♏	T ♐	S ♑	T ♒	F ♈	S ♉	W ♊	S ♌	M ♍	T ♏	S ♐	8.
T ♎	F ♐	F ♐	M ♑	W ♒	S ♈	M ♉	T ♋	S ♍	T ♎	F ♐	S ♑	9.
W ♏	S ♐	S ♐	T ♒	T ♓	S ♈	T ♊	F ♋	M ♍	W ♎	S ♐	M ♑	10.
T ♏	S ♐	S ♑	W ♒	F ♓	M ♉	W ♊	S ♌	T ♎	T ♏	S ♐	T ♒	11.
F ♏	M ♑	M ♑	T ♓	S ♈	T ♉	T ♋	S ♌	W ♎	F ♏	M ♑	W ♒	12.
S ♐	T ♑	T ♒	F ♓	S ♈	W ♊	F ♋	M ♍	T ♏	S ♐	T ♑	T ♒	13.
S ♐	W ♒	W ♒	S ♈	M ♉	T ♊	S ♌	T ♍	F ♏	S ♐	W ♒	F ♓	14.
M ♑	T ♒	T ♒	S ♈	T ♉	F ♋	S ♌	W ♎	S ♏	M ♑	T ♒	S ♓	15.
T ♑	F ♒	F ♓	M ♈	W ♊	S ♋	M ♍	T ♎	S ♐	T ♑	F ♒	S ♈	16.
W ♑	S ♓	S ♓	T ♉	T ♊	S ♌	T ♍	F ♏	M ♐	W ♑	S ♓	M ♈	17.
T ♒	S ♓	S ♈	W ♉	F ♋	M ♌	W ♎	S ♏	T ♑	T ♒	S ♓	T ♈	18.
F ♒	M ♈	M ♈	T ♊	S ♋	T ♍	T ♎	S ♐	W ♑	F ♒	M ♈	W ♉	19.
S ♓	T ♈	T ♈	F ♊	S ♌	W ♍	F ♎	M ♐	T ♒	S ♓	T ♈	T ♉	20.
S ♓	W ♉	W ♉	S ♋	M ♌	T ♎	S ♏	T ♐	F ♒	S ♓	W ♉	F ♊	21.
M ♈	T ♉	T ♉	S ♋	T ♌	F ♎	S ♏	W ♑	S ♒	M ♈	T ♉	S ♋	22.
T ♈	F ♉	F ♊	M ♌	W ♍	S ♏	M ♐	T ♑	S ♓	T ♈	F ♊	S ♋	23.
W ♈	S ♊	S ♊	T ♌	T ♍	S ♏	T ♐	F ♒	M ♓	W ♈	S ♊	M ♋	24.
T ♉	S ♊	S ♋	W ♍	F ♎	M ♏	W ♑	S ♒	T ♈	T ♉	S ♊	T ♌	25.
F ♉	M ♋	M ♋	T ♍	S ♎	T ♐	T ♑	S ♓	W ♈	F ♉	M ♋	W ♌	26.
S ♊	T ♋	T ♌	F ♍	S ♏	W ♐	F ♑	M ♓	T ♈	S ♊	T ♋	T ♍	27.
S ♊	W ♌	W ♌	S ♎	M ♏	T ♑	S ♒	T ♓	F ♉	S ♊	W ♌	F ♍	28.
M ♋		T ♍	S ♎	T ♐	F ♑	S ♒	W ♈	S ♉	M ♋	T ♌	S ♎	29.
T ♋		F ♍	M ♏	W ♐	S ♑	M ♓	T ♈	S ♊	T ♋	F ♍	S ♎	30.
W ♌		S ♎		T ♐		T ♓	F ♈		W ♋		M ♎	31.

2019

	January	February	March	April	May	June	July	August	September	October	November	December
1.	T ♏	F ♐	F ♑	M ♒	W ♓	S ♉	M ♊	T ♌	S ♎	T ♏	F ♐	S ♒
2.	W ♏	S ♑	S ♑	T ♓	T ♈	S ♉	T ♋	F ♌	M ♎	W ♏	S ♑	M ♒
3.	T ♐	S ♑	S ♒	W ♓	F ♈	M ♊	W ♋	S ♍	T ♏	T ♐	S ♑	T ♒
4.	F ♐	M ♒	M ♒	T ♈	S ♈	T ♊	T ♋	S ♍	W ♏	F ♐	M ♒	W ♓
5.	S ♑	T ♒	T ♒	F ♈	S ♉	W ♋	F ♌	M ♎	T ♏	S ♑	T ♒	T ♓
6.	S ♑	W ♒	W ♓	S ♈	M ♉	T ♋	S ♌	T ♎	F ♐	S ♑	W ♓	F ♈
7.	M ♑	T ♓	T ♓	S ♉	T ♊	F ♌	S ♍	W ♏	S ♐	M ♑	T ♓	S ♈
8.	T ♒	F ♓	F ♈	M ♉	W ♊	S ♌	M ♍	T ♏	S ♑	T ♒	F ♓	S ♈
9.	W ♒	S ♈	S ♈	T ♊	T ♋	S ♍	T ♎	F ♐	M ♑	W ♒	S ♈	M ♉
10.	T ♓	S ♈	S ♈	W ♊	F ♋	M ♍	W ♎	S ♐	T ♒	T ♓	S ♈	T ♉
11.	F ♓	M ♈	M ♉	T ♊	S ♌	T ♍	T ♏	S ♐	W ♒	F ♓	M ♉	W ♊
12.	S ♈	T ♉	T ♉	F ♋	S ♌	W ♎	F ♏	M ♑	T ♒	S ♓	T ♉	T ♊
13.	S ♈	W ♉	W ♊	S ♋	M ♍	T ♎	S ♐	T ♑	F ♓	S ♈	W ♉	F ♋
14.	M ♈	T ♊	T ♊	S ♌	T ♍	F ♏	S ♐	W ♒	S ♓	M ♈	T ♊	S ♋
15.	T ♉	F ♊	F ♋	M ♌	W ♎	S ♏	M ♑	T ♒	S ♈	T ♉	F ♊	S ♋
16.	W ♉	S ♋	S ♋	T ♍	T ♎	S ♐	T ♑	F ♒	M ♈	W ♉	S ♋	M ♌
17.	T ♉	S ♋	S ♋	W ♍	F ♏	M ♐	W ♑	S ♓	T ♈	T ♉	S ♌	T ♌
18.	F ♊	M ♌	M ♌	T ♎	S ♏	T ♑	T ♒	S ♓	W ♉	F ♊	M ♌	W ♍
19.	S ♊	T ♍	T ♌	F ♎	S ♏	W ♑	F ♒	M ♈	T ♉	S ♊	T ♌	T ♍
20.	S ♋	W ♍	W ♍	S ♏	M ♐	T ♑	S ♓	T ♈	F ♊	S ♋	W ♌	F ♎
21.	M ♌	T ♍	T ♎	S ♏	T ♐	F ♒	S ♓	W ♈	S ♊	M ♋	T ♍	S ♎
22.	T ♌	F ♎	F ♎	M ♐	W ♑	S ♒	M ♓	T ♉	S ♊	T ♌	F ♍	S ♏
23.	W ♌	S ♎	S ♎	T ♐	T ♑	S ♓	T ♈	F ♉	M ♋	W ♌	S ♎	M ♏
24.	T ♍	S ♏	S ♏	W ♑	F ♒	M ♓	W ♈	S ♊	T ♋	T ♍	S ♎	T ♐
25.	F ♍	M ♏	M ♏	T ♑	S ♒	T ♈	T ♉	S ♊	W ♌	F ♍	M ♏	W ♐
26.	S ♎	T ♐	T ♐	F ♑	S ♒	W ♈	F ♉	M ♋	T ♌	S ♎	T ♐	T ♑
27.	S ♎	W ♐	W ♐	S ♒	M ♓	T ♈	S ♉	T ♋	F ♍	S ♎	W ♐	F ♑
28.	M ♏	T ♐	T ♑	S ♒	T ♓	F ♉	S ♊	W ♌	S ♎	M ♏	T ♐	S ♑
29.	T ♏		F ♑	M ♓	W ♈	S ♉	M ♊	T ♌	S ♎	T ♏	F ♑	S ♒
30.	W ♐		S ♑	T ♓	T ♈	S ♊	T ♋	F ♍	M ♎	W ♐	S ♑	M ♒
31.	T ♐		S ♒		F ♈		W ♋	S ♍		T ♐		T ♓

2020

January	February	March	April	May	June	July	August	September	October	November	December	
W ♓	S ♈	S ♉	W ♋	F ♌	M ♎	W ♏	S ♑	T ♒	T ♈	S ♉	T ♊	1.
T ♓	S ♉	M ♊	T ♋	S ♌	T ♎	T ♏	S ♑	W ♓	F ♈	M ♉	W ♊	2.
F ♈	M ♉	T ♊	F ♌	S ♍	W ♏	F ♐	M ♒	T ♓	S ♈	T ♊	T ♋	3.
S ♈	T ♊	W ♊	S ♌	M ♍	T ♏	S ♐	T ♒	F ♈	S ♉	W ♊	F ♋	4.
S ♉	W ♊	T ♋	S ♍	T ♎	F ♐	S ♑	W ♒	S ♈	M ♉	T ♋	S ♌	5.
M ♉	T ♋	F ♋	M ♍	W ♎	S ♐	M ♑	T ♓	S ♈	T ♉	F ♋	S ♌	6.
T ♉	F ♋	S ♌	T ♎	T ♏	S ♑	T ♒	F ♓	M ♉	W ♊	S ♋	M ♍	7.
W ♊	S ♌	S ♌	W ♎	F ♏	M ♑	W ♒	S ♈	T ♉	T ♊	S ♌	T ♍	8.
T ♊	S ♌	M ♍	T ♏	S ♐	T ♑	T ♓	S ♈	W ♊	F ♋	M ♌	W ♍	9.
F ♋	M ♍	T ♍	F ♏	S ♐	W ♒	F ♓	M ♈	T ♊	S ♋	T ♍	T ♎	10.
S ♋	T ♍	W ♎	S ♐	M ♑	T ♒	S ♓	T ♉	F ♊	S ♋	W ♍	F ♎	11.
S ♌	W ♎	T ♎	S ♐	T ♑	F ♓	S ♈	W ♉	S ♋	M ♌	T ♎	S ♏	12.
M ♌	T ♎	F ♏	M ♐	W ♒	S ♓	M ♈	T ♊	S ♋	T ♌	F ♎	S ♏	13.
T ♍	F ♎	S ♏	T ♑	T ♒	S ♈	T ♉	F ♊	M ♌	W ♍	S ♏	M ♐	14.
W ♍	S ♏	S ♐	W ♑	F ♒	M ♈	W ♉	S ♋	T ♌	T ♍	S ♏	T ♐	15.
T ♎	S ♏	M ♐	T ♒	S ♓	T ♈	T ♉	S ♋	W ♍	F ♎	M ♐	W ♑	16.
F ♎	M ♐	T ♑	F ♒	S ♓	W ♉	F ♊	M ♋	T ♍	S ♎	T ♐	T ♑	17.
S ♏	T ♐	W ♑	S ♓	M ♈	T ♉	S ♊	T ♌	F ♎	S ♏	W ♑	F ♒	18.
S ♏	W ♑	T ♑	S ♓	T ♈	F ♊	S ♋	W ♌	S ♎	M ♏	T ♑	S ♒	19.
M ♐	T ♑	F ♒	M ♓	W ♈	S ♊	M ♋	T ♍	S ♏	T ♐	F ♒	S ♓	20.
T ♐	F ♒	S ♒	T ♈	T ♉	S ♋	T ♌	F ♍	M ♏	W ♐	S ♒	M ♓	21.
W ♐	S ♒	S ♓	W ♈	F ♊	M ♋	W ♌	S ♎	T ♐	T ♑	S ♒	T ♈	22.
T ♑	S ♓	M ♓	T ♈	S ♊	T ♋	T ♍	S ♎	W ♐	F ♑	M ♓	W ♈	23.
F ♒	M ♓	T ♈	F ♉	S ♊	W ♌	F ♍	M ♏	T ♑	S ♒	T ♓	T ♈	24.
S ♒	T ♓	W ♈	S ♉	M ♋	T ♌	S ♍	T ♏	F ♑	S ♒	W ♈	F ♉	25.
S ♒	W ♈	T ♈	S ♊	T ♋	F ♍	S ♎	W ♐	S ♑	M ♓	T ♈	S ♉	26.
M ♓	T ♈	F ♉	M ♊	W ♋	S ♍	M ♎	T ♐	S ♒	T ♓	F ♈	S ♊	27.
T ♓	F ♈	S ♉	T ♋	T ♌	S ♎	T ♏	F ♑	M ♒	W ♓	S ♉	M ♊	28.
W ♓	S ♉	S ♉	W ♋	F ♌	M ♎	W ♏	S ♑	T ♓	T ♈	S ♉	T ♊	29.
T ♈		M ♊	T ♋	S ♍	T ♏	T ♐	S ♑	W ♓	F ♈	M ♊	W ♋	30.
F ♈		T ♊		S ♍		F ♐	M ♒		S ♉		T ♋	31.

Index